8.95

DATE DUE

Flags
and Arms
across the
World

A field guide to the flags of the 174 nations of the world. National flags, coats of arms, state and provincial flags, presidential and ministerial banners—nearly 1,000 full-color illustrations, with maps, history, and thorough documentation.

Flags
and Arms
across the
World

Whitney Smith

Executive Director
Flag Research Center, Winchester,
Massachusetts

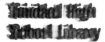
McGraw-Hill Book Company

New York   St. Louis   San Francisco

CONTENTS

FOR ANNE

A McGraw-Hill Co-Publication
Copyright © 1980 by
McGraw-Hill Book Company
(UK) Limited, Maidenhead,
England. All rights reserved.
No part of this publication
may be reproduced, stored in
a retrieval system, or transmit-
ted in any form or by any
means, electronic, mechani-
cal, photocopying, recording,
or otherwise, without the
prior written permission of
the publisher.

Library of Congress Catalog-
ing in Publication Data

Smith, Whitney.
    Flags and arms across the
world.
    Revision of a section of
Flags through the ages and
across the world.
    Includes index.
    1. Flags. I. Smith, Whitney.
Flags through the ages and
across the world. II. Title.
JC345.S56   929.9
79-13271

ISBN 0-07-059094-X

Artwork by:
ALFRED ZNAMIEROWSKI

Printed and bound by:
Brepols, Turnhout, Belgium
Composition by:
Weber AG, Biel, Switzerland

Printed in Belgium

INTRODUCTION

Flags have practical uses, but their primary function has always been social communication. National flags in particular stimulate the viewer to feel and act in a calculated way. They represent or identify the existence, presence, origin, authority, possession, loyalty, glory, beliefs, objectives, and status of an entire nation. They are employed to honor and dishonor, warn and encourage, threaten and promise, exalt and condemn, commemorate and deny. They remind and incite and defy the child in school, the soldier, the voter, the enemy, the ally, and the stranger. Flags authenticate claims, dramatize political demands, establish a common framework within which likeminded nations are willing to work out mutually agreeable solutions—or postulate and maintain irreconcilable differences that prevent agreements from occuring. It is scarcely possible to conceive of the world, of human society, without flags.

This is particularly true in the modern era when the world is organized into a definite number of nation-states. International corporations; ideologies; religions; and social and economic class distinctions are important in the everyday life of individuals and in great political movements, yet none of these has deterred the growth of nationalism and many have reinforced the nation-state. Because flags constitute explicit self-analysis by nation-states, vexillology, the study of flag history and symbolism, may justly claim to be an auxiliary to the social sciences.

If it is true that a flag is a piece of colored cloth for which men and women are willing to fight and even die, a knowledge of flags can give us some insights into the countries that fly them. Despite marked differences, the Scandinavian lands have common interests reflected in similar flag designs. Fierce regional loyalties are reflected in the flags of subdivisions in Spain and the United States, while there are clearly marked limits to expressions of regionalism shown in the flags of the Yugoslav republics and Liberian counties. The United Kingdom and Malaysia mark changes in their constituent parts by corresponding changes in the national flag. Dozens of countries suggest through their symbols the importance of agriculture as the livelihood of the people and industrialization as the hope of the future. Other flags and arms suggest the lineage of a ruling dynasty (Liechtenstein), lost territories eventually to be regained for the fatherland (Somalia), the role of the United Nations in leading the country to independence (Western Samoa), and distinctive local flora and fauna (Canada, Dominica).

Because flags are flown on ships and buildings, hoisted in battle and on mountaintops, carried to the Olympic Games and to outer space, flaunted in sports events and in political rallies, they are the primary symbols of the modern age. Coats of arms are less extensively used because they are less flexible, generally appearing in painted, printed, or sculpted form to identify an agency or instrument of a government. Nevertheless their rich graphic compositions and their use on flags make arms significant sources of information about nation-states. Many conform to the traditional rules of heraldry, which evolved in the Middle Ages in Europe and was spread by European imperialism to all parts of the world. On the other hand many arms have made a sharp break from heraldic tradition, although their distinctive forms fulfill the same functions.

Both heraldry and vexillology have specialized terminology useful in making technical descriptions. By and large this terminology has been avoided in the present book, which emphasizes the symbolic and historic aspects of these symbols. Nevertheless many readers will find the need or desire for further information not only on terminology but other aspects of flags—such as the rules of etiquette which have developed regulating their usage. There are also vast areas of flag lore and heraldry not touched upon in this volume—symbols of political parties, religions, and cities; the use of flags at sea by yacht clubs and shipping companies or as a means of signaling; the diverse forms and ceremonies associated with military banners; the origins and development of heraldry in Europe and Japan; the interrelationship between flags, arms, and seals. Some suggestions are provided on page 8 of this book for further reading.

The study of flags and state heraldry is by no means a matter only of dusty archives, long forgotten heroes and incidents: these symbols reflect political realities and therefore change as profoundly and frequently as nation-states themselves. Precisely that dynamism has served as a major reason for the creation of flag study societies, linked since 1967 in the International Federation of Vexillological Associations. Each organization has activities of its own; the Federation sponsors a biennial congress. Its official journal, *The Flag Bulletin,* is published by the Flag Research Center (Winchester, Mass. 01890 USA)—the oldest and largest institution in the world dedicated to vexillology. Those who have questions or comments or criticisms concerning any aspect of this book or who wish to make contact with other vexillologists are invited to write to the author, who is Executive Director of the Center. In turn he would like to take this opportunity to extend his profound thanks to the hundreds of colleagues, government officials, librarians, and others who over the years have assisted in making this book possible. The lack of space to list their names in no way diminishes the gratitude the author owes them.

Whether or not the reader finds sufficient inspiration from this book to join in the growing world of vexillology, may he or she in finishing the book at least concur with a comment made by Henri Châtelaine in 1720 when he described vexillology as "an intriguing and fascinating study not only for those who sail or live in maritime cities, but as well for all who are inquisitive."

Dr. Whitney Smith
Flag Research Center, Winchester, Mass. USA

MORE ABOUT FLAGS AND ARMS

For the reader who is looking for information on flag terminology, the history of flags, flag etiquette, flag symbols, and a list of sources on flags and arms for all nations, the best single book is *Flags Through the Ages and Across the World* by Whitney Smith (New York, etc.: McGraw Hill, 1975; available in English, French, German, Dutch, Italian, Danish, and Japanese).

Flags and arms are constantly changing; to keep up to date, the best single source is the bimonthly illustrated

Flag Bulletin published by the Flag Research Center, Winchester, Mass. 01890 USA, which also has articles on other aspects of flags, past and present. A complete listing of other journals and newsletters relating to flags and state heraldry is available from the Flag Research Center. Since 1965 the International Federation of Vexillological Associations (of which *The Flag Bulletin* is the official journal) has held biennial International Congresses of Vexillology whose published reports are important for those who want to know about flags.

Other general sources of information include *Flags of the World* by E.M.C. Barraclough and W.G. Crampton (London: Warne, 1978); *The International Flag Book In Color* by Christian Pedersen (New York: Morrow, 1971); *Wappenbilder Lexikon* by Ottfried Neubecker and Wilhelm Rentzmann (Munich: Battenberg, 1974); and *The Bibliography of Flags of Foreign Nations* by Whitney Smith (Boston: G.K. Hall, 1965).

There are more specialized books which nevertheless have a great deal of information on flags other than those suggested by their titles—*British Flags* by W.G. Perrin (Cambridge: University Press, 1922); *The Flag Book of the United States* by Whitney Smith (New York: Morrow, 1975); *Vor- und Frühgeschichte des europäischen Flaggenwesens* by Hans Horstmann (Bremen: Schünemann, 1971); *dtv-Lexikon politischer Symbole* (Munich: dtv 1970) by Arnold Rabbow; and *Military Flags of the World 1618–1900* by Terence Wise (New York: Arco, 1978).

SYMBOLS USED IN THIS BOOK

The design and color characteristics of each flag are evident in the illustration; its history and symbolism are set forth in the accompanying text. Nevertheless there are important aspects of flags—their proportions and usage, for example—which should be available for ready reference but which take up text space unnecessarily if written out. For this reason a system of symbols, including a grid pattern to indicate usage, has been developed to provide accurate, internationally comprehensible, succinct data. These symbols are explained on the opposite page.

It should be noted that some countries have more than one "national flag"; a few countries have as many as four or five different designs serving as a national flag under different circumstances. The main flag shown for each country in this book is the civil flag, i.e. the one flown on land by private citizens. If no such flag exists, the state flag (i.e. the one flown on public buildings) is shown. The other types of national flags identified by the grid pattern (war flag, civil ensign, state ensign, war ensign) are used under different circumstances. The same grid pattern is used for the flags of subdivisions and dependencies, although these flags are normally flown subordinate to the national flag(s) of the country in question.

The simplest way to understand the grid pattern is to recall that a dot above the horizontal line means use on land; one below the line means use at sea. From left to right the three vertical columns stand for use by private persons, by the government, and by the military.

NATIONAL FLAGS/IDENTIFICATION SYMBOLS.

The following international standard symbols are used to indicate the functions of a particular flag, its proportions, or some other significant fact about it.

	PRIVATE USE	PUBLIC USE	MILITARY USE
	CIVIL	STATE	WAR
USE ON LAND	FLAG	FLAG	FLAG
USE AT SEA	CIVIL ENSIGN	STATE ENSIGN	WAR ENSIGN

- CIVIL FLAG
- STATE FLAG
- WAR FLAG
- CIVIL ENSIGN
- STATE ENSIGN
- WAR ENSIGN
- CIVIL AND STATE FLAG
- STATE AND WAR FLAG
- CIVIL AND STATE ENSIGN
- STATE AND WAR ENSIGN
- CIVIL FLAG AND ENSIGN
- STATE FLAG AND ENSIGN
- WAR FLAG AND ENSIGN
- NATIONAL FLAG
- NATIONAL ENSIGN
- WAR FLAG AND ENSIGN, STATE FLAG
- STATE FLAG, CIVIL AND WAR ENSIGN
- CIVIL AND STATE FLAG AND ENSIGN
- STATE AND WAR FLAG AND ENSIGN
- NATIONAL FLAG, STATE ENSIGN
- NATIONAL FLAG, CIVIL AND STATE ENSIGN
- NATIONAL ENSIGN, STATE AND WAR FLAG
- CIVIL AND STATE FLAG, NATIONAL ENSIGN
- NATIONAL FLAG AND ENSIGN

- PROPOSAL
  (design never actually used)
- RECONSTRUCTED
  (design based on written sources only)
- REVERSE
  (design shown is reverse side of flag)
- VARIANT
  (one of two or more variants of the same basic design)
- ALTERNATE
  (one of two flags used simultaneously — or under special conditions — for the same function)
- 1:2 OFFICIAL PROPORTIONS
- 1:2≈ UNOFFICIAL PROPORTIONS
  (de facto or unknown, but approximate)
- DE FACTO
  (in actual use but without legal sanction)
- TWO-SIDED
  (reverse side is unlike design shown)
- SINISTER HOIST
  (The obverse or more important side of the flag is seen when the hoist is shown to the observer's right.)

INDEX OF COUNTRIES

The nations are arranged alphabetically in this book by their official name in their language, and a number is assigned to each. The English-language index below gives the locator-number for each nation.

12

El Salvador	48	Indonesia	69
Equatorial Guinea	60	Iran	70
Ethiopia	51	Iraq	71
		Ireland	47
Faroes	53	Israel	73
Fiji	52	Italy	74
Finland	148	Ivory Coast	36
France	54		
		Jamaica	75
Gabon	55	Japan	115
The Gambia	56	Jordan	116
Germany	39		
Germany	40	Kampuchea	77
Ghana	57	Kenya	78
Greece	66	Kiribati	79
Grenada	58	Korea	80
Guatemala	59	Korea	81
Guinea	62	Kuwait	83
Guinea-Bissau	61		
Guyana	63	Laos	84
		Lebanon	89
Haiti	64	Lesotho	85
Honduras	68	Liberia	86
Hungary	92	Libya	87
		Liechtenstein	88
Iceland	72	Luxembourg	90
India	16		

13

STATE ARMS

On 27 April 1978 a revolution set Afghanistan on the road to a Marxist-Leninist state. This is reflected in its red flag and the national coat of arms which appears on that flag.

The five-pointed star at the top of the arms is said to stand for the five nationalities of the country. The Pushto word in the center means ''the

1:2

Officially hoisted
19 October 1978.

masses'' and the red color of the flag symbolizes their struggle against imperialism, feudalism, and other forms of oppression.

The inscription on the ribbon reads ''Saur Revolution 1357''—that is, April Revolution 1978. The wreath of wheat not only suggests the agricultural pursuits of most of the population, but recalls the tradition that the legendary first Aryan king, Yama, and the first Afghan king, Ahmad Shah, were crowned with wheat.

1:2

Afghanistan has an unusual ''decorative flag'' which is displayed vertically.

AL AMIRAT AL ARABIYAH
AL MUTAHIDAH

UNITED ARAB
EMIRATES

PERSIAN GULF   IRAN

★ Abu Dhabi

OMAN

SAUDI ARABIA

STATE ARMS

The United Arab Emirates chose the
four recognized pan-Arab colors for
its national flag. The red and white
flags of its states are variations of a
single design first used in 1820 (see
Bahrain).

The Arab Revolt Flag was adopted by
King Husain of the Hijaz in 1917. The
green, white, and black colors had

1:2

Officially hoisted
2 December 1971.

For centuries hunting with the
falcon has been a popular sport
among the wealthy in the Persian
Gulf area. It is not suprising
therefore to find this bird and the
familiar *dhow*—the ship in which
Arabs for centuries have sailed
the Indian Ocean—included with
the name of the state in the arms
of the United Arab Emirates. The
design is apparently based on the
arms of its largest member state,
Abu Dhabi.

been developed three years earlier by
young Arabs opposed to Ottoman rule.
They symbolized three historic Arab
dynasties—the Fatimids (green),
Abbassids (black), and the Ummayads
(white). To this was added red, the
color of the sherifs of Mecca and
hence of Husain himself.

The original Arab Revolt Flag had
horizontal stripes of black over green
over white with a red triangle at the
hoist. Over the years there have been
many variations of the original flag,
including the one adopted by the
United Arab Emirates.

17

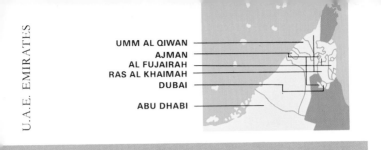

UMM AL QIWAN
AJMAN
AL FUJAIRAH
RAS AL KHAIMAH
DUBAI

ABU DHABI

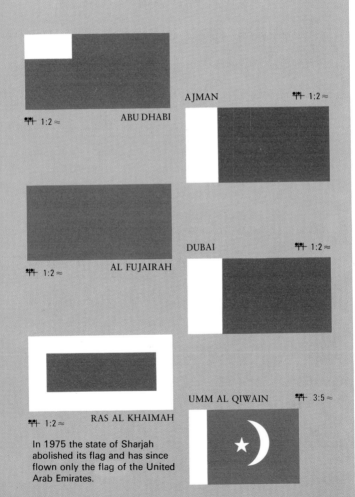

1:2 ≈   ABU DHABI

AJMAN   1:2 ≈

1:2 ≈   AL FUJAIRAH

DUBAI   1:2 ≈

1:2 ≈   RAS AL KHAIMAH

UMM AL QIWAIN   3:5 ≈

In 1975 the state of Sharjah abolished its flag and has since flown only the flag of the United Arab Emirates.

18

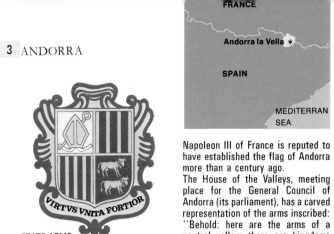

STATE ARMS

Napoleon III of France is reputed to have established the flag of Andorra more than a century ago.

The House of the Valleys, meeting place for the General Council of Andorra (its parliament), has a carved representation of the arms inscribed: "Behold: here are the arms of a neutral valley; there are kingdoms

Usage initiated
ca. 1866.

⚓ 2:3 ▱

⚓ 2:3 (▱) ▱

Andorra is often referred to as a republic or as a principality. In the modern sense of these words, neither one is appropriate.

Andorra is rather a condominium ruled jointly by Spain and France.

more noble by which they rejoice to be guarded. If individually they bless other peoples, Andorra, why should they not, joined, bring to you a golden age?"

The arms of Andorra express its history well. The crozier and miter are symbols of the bishops of Urgel; their authority was challenged by the counts of Foix—whose arms appear in the second quarter of the shield. In 1278 the two became joint rulers of Andorra.

The arms of Catalonia and of Béarn figure in the third and fourth quarters of Andorra's shield. The motto may be translated from the Latin, "Strength United is Stronger."

STATE ARMS

The five points in the star of the national flag stand for unity, liberty, justice, democracy, and progress. The star itself is as an emblem of internationalism and progress. These are based on the unity of industrial and agricultural laborers, respectively symbolized in the flag by the cogwheel and machete.

Officially hoisted 11 November 1975.

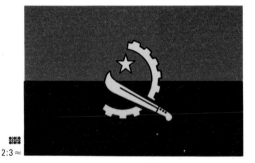

2:3 ≈

In the development of the new nation (symbolized by the rising sun in the coat of arms) the importance of education and culture has been suggested by an open book. Workers and peasants are represented by the emblems of industry and agriculture which surround the arms—a cogwheel and corn, coffee, and cotton. The arms also bear a hoe for labor and a machete, indicating the armed struggle which liberated the country from the Portuguese.

Angola salutes the African continent in the black stripe of its flag and recalls in the red stripe both the oppression of past colonial rule and the liberation struggle which eventually ended that era. The Popular Movement for the Liberation of Angola, which provided the ideology and leadership that eventually culminated in independence, displayed a flag of red over black horizontal stripes, but in the center was simply a large yellow five-pointed star. That flag was adopted in 1965 and continues to be used by the party.

STATE ARMS

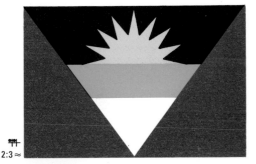

Officially
hoisted
27 February
1967.

2:3 ≈

Reginald Samuel was the winner among 600 entrants in a competition to design the Antiguan flag. He saw the red field as standing for the dynamism of the people and its V shape as a symbol of victory. Black for the soil and the African heritage of the people form a background for the golden sun of a new era. Blue stands for hope. Together the yellow, blue, and white indicate the sun, sea, and sand which make the island an attraction for tourism.

The coat of arms was developed by Gordon Christopher. Its sugar cane and sugar mill recall the former chief industry of the island. Other elements include sea island cotton, the pineapple, and the crimson hibiscus.

The deer which are hunted on the island of Barbuda, a part of Antigua, serve as supporters to the shield. The motto was suggested by James H. Carrott of the Ministry of Trade, Production, and Labor.

1:2

In 1967 Antigua became an Associated State. Self-governing in all matters except defense and foreign affairs, it is now (April 1979) planning for a transition to complete independence shortly.

AL ARABIYAH AL SAUDIYAH SAUDI ARABIA

STATE ARMS

Green, long symbolic in Islam as the color of the Fatimid dynasty established by the Prophet's daughter, Fatima, was used by early Muslims as a flag. A green turban belonging to the Prophet supposedly was their first such flag.

Abd al-Aziz ibn Saud, leader of the Wahabis (a strict Muslim sect), ex-

Officially adopted 15 March 1973.

2:3

2:3

ROYAL FLAG

tended their rule throughout the heartland of Arabia, renaming the country after himself in 1932.

The traditional Wahabi banner is now the official Saudi state flag. It displays the *Shahada* or Word of Unity of Islam: "There is no god but Allah; Muhammad is the Prophet of Allah." The sword, a symbol of Islamic justice and righteousness, is repeated in the coat of arms which also includes a date palm representing patience and endurance.

Because of the sacred character of its inscription, the flag of Saudi Arabia is never half-staffed for any reason. The design, moreover, is sewn so that it reads correctly on both sides of the flag.

STATE ARMS

A military color hoisted by General Manuel Belgrano on 12 February 1812 in the city of Rosario is hailed by Argentines as their first national flag. Nevertheless the colors of that flag date back two years before that. Cockades of celeste and white were distributed to the crowds which gathered on 25 May 1810 in the Plaza of

Officially adopted 25 July 1816.

2:3 ≈

2:3

Buenos Aires. They successfully demanded from the Spanish viceroy the creation of a popular local government.

The day had been cloudy and the people took it as a favorable omen when the clouds parted and the sun shone down upon them. That "Sun of May" came to be recognized as a national symbol.

It was added to the celeste-white-celeste civil flag in 1818, forming the state flag still in use today.

Over the years there has been disagreement on what the shade of blue in the Argentine flag should be called and what exactly it should look like.

PRESIDENTIAL FLAG   3:4

23

STATE ARMS

In 1854 gold miners at the Eureka Stockade in Victoria revolted against corrupt police, limited suffrage, and other political and economic injustices. Their flag was blue with five eight-pointed white stars on a white cross, symbolizing the sky which is common to all men, and hope and liberty. That flag inspired many sub-

1:2

Officially adopted 22 May 1909; confirmed in present form 15 April 1954.

1:2

1:2

24

sequent designs.

Unification of six British colonies in the Commonwealth of Australia on 1 January 1901 called for a national flag. Chosen in a competition which drew more than 30,000 entries, this flag displays the Southern Cross constellation reminiscent of the Eureka Stockade flag. In addition a seven-pointed star (changed from six points in 1909) represents the Commonwealth with its six states and its territories. The Union Jack is a reminder of the historical and political links which Australia has with Britain.

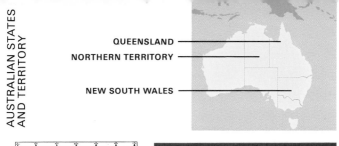

AUSTRALIAN STATES AND TERRITORY

QUEENSLAND
NORTHERN TERRITORY
NEW SOUTH WALES

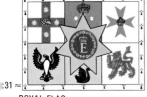

≈31

ROYAL FLAG

GOVERNOR-GENERAL'S FLAG

NEW SOUTH WALES
Officially adopted
15 February 1876.

1:2

NORTHERN TERRITORY
Officially hoisted
1 July 1978.

1:2

QUEENSLAND
Officially adopted
29 November 1876.

1:2

WESTERN AUSTRALIA ——————
SOUTH AUSTRALIA ——————
VICTORIA ——————
TASMANIA ——————

SOUTH AUSTRALIA
Officially adopted
13 January 1904.

1:2

TASMANIA
Officially adopted
25 September 1876.

1:2

VICTORIA
Officially adopted
30 November 1877.

1:2

WESTERN AUSTRALIA
Officially adopted
27 November 1875.

1:2

ATLANTIC OCEAN

FLORIDA

✴ **Nassau**

CUBA

STATE ARMS

The golden sands of the 700 Bahamian islands are reflected in the center stripe of the flag, while the aquamarine stripes bring to mind the various shades of ocean waters around those islands. The black triangle indicates the unity of the Bahamian people and their determination to develop the resources of ▶ P. 248

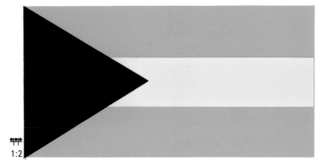

1:2

Officially hoisted 10 July 1973.

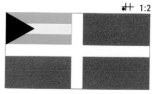

⌗⊢ 1:2

GOVERNOR-GENERAL'S FLAG

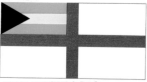

⊣⌗ 1:2 ⊡

PRIME MINISTER'S FLAG

1:2

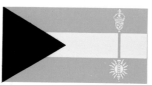

1:2

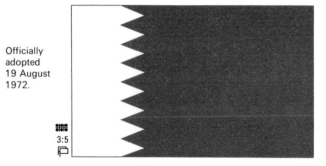

STATE ARMS

Article III of the General Treaty signed in 1820 by the British and certain states of the Persian Gulf required that ''the friendly Arabs should carry by land and sea a red flag, with or without letters in it, at their option, and this shall be in a border of white....''

Bahrain, one of the signatories to the

Officially
adopted
19 August
1972.

3:5

3:5

Two versions of the national flag are officially recognized. In practice the serrated design is preferred, although there is no special significance to either pattern.

treaty, still flies an adaptation of that flag today. Like the others—now parts of the United Arab Emirates—Bahrain has made modifications in the original design. The border now runs only along the hoist edge of the flag and the flag itself is no longer square. The red color was originally a symbol of the Kharijite Muslims of the area, white having been added as a symbol of the peace established in an area formerly characterized by frequent warfare.

The coat of arms developed in the 1930s by a British adviser to the sheikh, Sir Charles Belgrave, is based on the national flag.

STATE ARMS

For almost a quarter of a century Pakistan consisted of two parts separated by Indian territory—as well as by language, economic conditions, and culture. Finally in 1971 East Pakistan proclaimed its independence as Bangladesh. The green of the new flag may have been inspired by its associations with Islam. During the

Officially confirmed 25 January 1972.

3:5

– 1:2

Jute, padi, and a water lily (shapla flower) appear in the Bangladesh coat of arms. Bengali rivers and the social and economic goals of the country are reflected in its wavy lines and four stars.

independence struggle a silhouette map of Bangladesh appeared in gold on the disk; this was later omitted because of difficulties in properly representing it on both sides of the flag.

The verdure of the land is symbolized by the field of the flag; blood shed in the battle for freedom is recalled by the red disk. The flag was designed by Serajul Alam, whose name means "Light of the Flag."

The disk is set slightly toward the hoist so that when the flag is flying it will appear to be in the center.

29

DOMINICAN
REPUBLIC PUERTO   ATLANTIC
            RICO   OCEAN

CARIBBEAN SEA

Bridgetown ✶

SOUTH AMERICA

STATE ARMS

Under British colonial rule the badge of Barbados included a trident, the traditional symbol of the sea god Neptune. Use of a trident in the national flag thus reflects the nation's past and its association with the sea. The fact that the trident head has been broken from its shaft indicates a break with the colonial past.

Officially hoisted
30 November
1966.

2:3

GOVERNOR-GENERAL'S FLAG   3:4≈

PRIME MINISTER'S FLAG   2:3≈

The sea and sky surrounding the island are represented by the blue stripes of the flag, its sandy beaches by the gold stripe. Grantley Prescod chose the colors and designed the flag for which he won first prize in a nationwide competition.

A royal warrant dated 21 December 1965 confirmed the arms of Barbados. Its shield includes a bearded fig tree and two flowers known as the red pride of Barbados. The arm in the crest holds sugar cane, an important agricultural resource for Barbados. The dexter supporter is a dolphin rendered in a stylized heraldic form.

13 BELGIQUE/BELGIË
BELGIUM

NORTH SEA

GREAT BRITAIN

NETHERLANDS

GERMANY, F.R.

* Brussels

FRANCE

STATE AND ROYAL ARMS

Officially adopted
23 January 1831.

Long heraldic traditions—still evident in the armorial banners of Belgian provinces—emphasize the colors red, gold, and black. The arms of Brabant were the specific inspiration for the choice of those colors in the national flag.

During the unsuccessful revolt of 1789 against Austrian rule, the three ▶ P. 248

13:15 ≈

⊞ 2:3 ≈

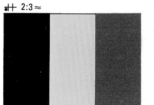

⊞ 2:3

⊞ 2:3

1:1   ROYAL FLAG

31

BELGIAN PROVINCES

WEST FLANDERS
ANTWERP
EAST FLANDERS
BRABANT
LIMBURG
LIEGE
HAINAUT
NAMUR
LUXEMBOURG

VLAANDEREN
FLANDERS

1:1 ≈

WALLONIE
WALLONIA

1:1 ≈

ANTWERPEN
ANTWERP

1:1 ≈

BRABANT

1:1 ≈

HAINAUT

1:1 ≈

LIÈGE

1:1 ≈

LIMBOURG

1:1 ≈

LUXEMBOURG

1:1 ≈

NAMUR
32

OOST-VLAANDEREN
EAST FLANDERS

1:1 ≈

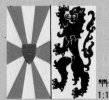

WEST-VLAANDEREN
WEST FLANDERS

MEXICO

Belmopan *

CARIBBEAN SEA

GUATEMALA

HONDURAS

STATE ARMS

Since neighboring Guatemala claims the territory of Belize as its own, concern for its borders has so far prevented Belize from seeking complete independence from Great Britain. Internally self-governing, it has an unofficial flag which is promoted by the ruling People's United Party. It has been in actual use for a ▶ P. 248

Officially hoisted 2 February 1950.

2:3

GOVERNOR-GENERAL'S FLAG

 1:2

1:2

1:2

PREMIER'S FLAG

2:3 ≈

33

STATE ARMS

From the 15th through the 17th century a powerful empire called Benin existed on the coast of the Gulf of Guinea. The name was resurrected in 1975 for what had formerly been the Republic of Dahomey.

The flag of Benin expresses in its green field the agricultural base of the national economy. The red star is

Officially hoisted
1 December 1975.

2:3

officially said to "symbolize national unity, the union of all the revolutionary forces to conquer the enemies within and without and to create a new, revolutionary, and socialist Benin nation." The revolutionary symbolism of the star and its color is found in many countries of Europe and Asia.

The Marxist-Leninist program of Benin was proclaimed by President Mathieu Kerekou in December 1974. The sole political organization of the country, the Party of the People's Revolution of Benin, has a flag exactly like the Benin national flag— except that the colors are reversed.

The arms include symbols of agriculture (ears of corn and a pile of corn stalks) and industry (a cogwheel), the initials of the country's name in French, and the design of the national flag.

सत्यमेव जयते

STATE ARMS

In the third century B.C. Asoka ruled the Maurya Empire, covering much of the Indian peninsula. Among the architectural monuments remaining from his rule is a pillar whose capital today serves as the state arms of India. (Written below the capital is a quotation from the ancient *Mundaka Upanishad*, reading "Truth Alone

Officially adopted
22 July 1947.

2:3

Triumphs.") The animals of this capital are Buddhist symbols, but the wheel is even more important in embodying the principles of that religion.

The same wheel is emblazoned on the Indian national flag. It was substituted for the spinning wheel in the flag of the Congress Party which had led the independence struggle. That emblem stood for the party's struggle to encourage self-reliance, productive labor, nonviolence, and a sense of personal participation in the independence struggle by even the poorest citizens.

In 1920 the colors red and green, to represent the Hindu and Muslim religious communities, had been sug-

Because it formerly had a special status, Jammu and Kashmir alone of the Indian states has a distinctive flag of its own. The three stripes stand for the districts, the red color for labor.

JAMMU AND KASHMIR

2:3

35

1:2

 2:3

 2:3

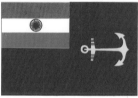

 2:3 ≈

gested for a Congress flag. Party leader Mohandas Gandhi revised the flag to white-green-red horizontal stripes with the spinning wheel. White was to stand for the minority religious groups. That flag became very popular. In Nagpur in 1923 British authorities took its display as a provocation and challenged the right of Indian nationalists to display their flag wherever they wished. The latter responded with peaceful demonstrations involving thousands who carried the flag in relay for two months.

There was dissatisfaction, however, because some saw the colors emphasizing divisions within the Indian population rather than the unity necessary for achieving common goals. Since the 1920 flag had not been officially adopted, a committee was appointed in 1931 to examine the question. It proposed a flag of saffron-white-green with the spinning wheel in the center. The official interpretation of the colors explained them as symbols of courage and sacrifice, peace and truth, and faith and chivalry.

This flag was adopted in August 1933 and extensively used. The Free India movement, led by Subhas Chandra Bose under Japanese sponsorship, hoisted a plain tricolor of saffron-white-green in 1943–1944.

STATE ARMS

The independence of Bolivia was originally achieved in 1825 through the military victories of leaders from the north, Bolivar and Sucre. The horizontal stripes and the colors yellow and red of the flag were undoubtedly influenced by those already existing in Colombia.

Manuel Belzú, the first president of

Officially adopted 14 July 1888.

2:3

2:3

Bolivia to base his power on the Indian majority, established the flag in 1851 in basically the same form as used today. The red has been interpreted as signifying the valor of the Bolivian soldier, green the fertility of the land, and gold the richness of national mineral resources.

Its agricultural and mineral wealth are reflected in the coat of arms by the wheat sheaf, breadfruit tree, and the argentiferous Mount Potosí. Native fauna—the condor and alpaca—are also included. The sun is an ancient Inca symbol.

3:4 ≈

37

TSHWARAGANANG LO DIRE PULA E NE

STATE ARMS

The leopard is used among the Tswana as a symbol of supreme authority. In the past only a chief was allowed to wear a leopard skin, and the ceremonial mace of the national parliament has a carved leopard at the top.

In the Bophuthatswana arms officially established on 8 September 1972,

Officially adopted 19 April 1973.

2:3

leopards serve as supporters. Authority to lead the people in developing the nation is symbolized by the face of a leopard in the national flag, while its orange stripe stands for the golden path to be taken toward that end. Finally, the blue of the flag is a reminder of the infinite heavens and the limitless efforts people must exert in transforming the nation.

The flag, drafted jointly by members of the Executive Council of the Bophuthatswana Legislative Assembly and South African heraldic experts, flew subordinate to the flag of South Africa until the proclamation of independence on 6 December 1977.

The South African government has created separate states for the black peoples within its borders. Independence has been granted so far to two such states, Bophuthatswana and Transkei, although they are still economically dependent on South Africa and have not received diplomatic recognition from any other country. Blacks of Tswana and Xhosa ancestry respectively are considered citizens of these states, even if for generations they have lived elsewhere and consider themselves to be South Africans.

19 BOTSWANA

NAMIBIA

ATLANTIC OCEAN

Gaborone *

SOUTH AFRICA

INDIAN OCEAN

STATE ARMS

In submitting the Botswana flag and arms for legislative approval, Prime Minister Dr. Seretse Khama explained: "Rain is our lifeblood, and *'pula'* is a well-known expression which means more than just 'rain'. It expresses a hope and a belief that we will win through in the end and good fortune will be our partner in the

Officially
hoisted
30 September
1966.

2:3

PRESIDENTIAL FLAG

15:23

years ahead." The blue field of the flag was chosen to represent water as well as the sky. The coat of arms features the traditional heraldic representation of water and includes the Tswana word for rain.

The black and white stripes of the flag and the zebras reflect a determination to build a society of equal opportunity for persons of all races. The bull's head is an emblem of the livestock industry. Cogwheels suggest the desire for industrialization; the stalk of sorghum recalls that the national economy is still primarily agricultural.

STATE ARMS

The green of this vast land and its golden mineral wealth are represented in the Brazilian flag, whose diamond shape recalls many French military colors of the early 19th century. A similar flag was adopted by Brazil in 1822 upon gaining independence from Portugal.

The historic colors of Portugal, blue

Officially adopted 30 May 1968.

7:10

PRESIDENTIAL FLAG

2:3≈

The arms include the date on which the Brazilian empire was replaced by a republic.
Surrounding the central emblem are branches of coffee and tobacco.

and white, appear in the Brazilian flag. The globe shows the constellations as they appear over Rio de Janeiro, but in mirror image. The motto ''Order and Progress'' is a Positivist slogan.

Unlike the geometric arrangement in the United States flag, Brazil's stars correspond to actual constellations. Each individual star corresponds to a specific state (plus one star for all the territories), whereas in the American flag the stars represent the states collectively. Each Brazilian star is one of five different sizes, rather than all being the same.

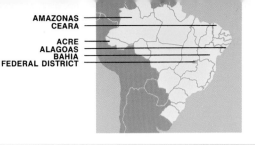

AMAZONAS
CEARA

ACRE
ALAGOAS
BAHIA
FEDERAL DISTRICT

20

ACRE
Officially confirmed 1 March 1963.

ALAGOAS
Off. adopted 23 September 1963.

4:7 ≈

AMAZONAS
Usage initiated ca. 1897.

7:10 ≈

BAHIA
Usage initiated 26 May 1889.

7:10 ≈

CEARÁ
Officially adopted ca. 31 August 1967.

7:10

DISTRITO FEDERAL
FEDERAL DISTRICT
Off. hoisted 7 September 1969.

13:18

41

TRABALHA E CONFIA

7:10

ESPÍRITO SANTO
Officially adopted 24 April 1947.

GOIÁS
Usage initiated 30 July 1919.

7:10 ≈

MARANHÃO
Officially confirmed 1 December 1971.

2:3

MATO GROSSO
Officially confirmed 11 July 1947.

MINAS GERAIS
Officially adopted 27 November 1962.

LIBERTAS QUÆ SERA
TAMEN

7:10 ≈

7:10 ≈

MATO GROSSO DO SUL
Officially adopted 1 January 1979.

7:10

7:10 ≈

PARÁ
Usage initiated 17 November 1889.

PARAÍBA
Officially hoisted 27 October 1965.

7:10

PARANÁ
Officially adopted 31 March 1947.

2:3

PERNAMBUCO
Usage initiated 23 February 1917.

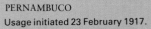

7:10 ≈

PIAUÍ
Usage initiated 24 July 1922.

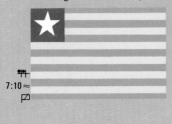

7:10 ≈

RIO DE JANEIRO
Usage initiated ca. 1947.

7:10 ≈

43

RIO GRANDE DO NORTE
SERGIPE
SAO PAULO
SANTA CATARINA
RIO GRANDE DO SUL

2:3

RIO GRANDE DO NORTE
Officially adopted 3 December 1957.

RIO GRANDE DO SUL
Usage confirmed 1947.

7:10 ≈

SANTA CATARINA
Officially adopted 23 October 1953.

3:4

SÃO PAULO
Officially adopted 3 September 1948.

7:10 ≈

SERGIPE
Usage initiated ca. 1947.

2:3 ≈

Historic revolutionary banners
and the national flag of the
United States are among the
design sources for the Brazilian
state flags. All the state flags
were outlawed by the Brazilian
constitution of 10 November
1937. The constitution of 18
September 1946 again permitted
the use of state symbols.

STATE ARMS

In 1906 when Brunei became a British protected state, a national flag was designed. To the plain yellow flag previously used as a symbol of the sultan, white and black stripes were added to represent the two leading *wazirs* (state advisers), the Pengiran Bendahara and the Pengiran Pemancha.

1:2

Officially adopted late 1959.

In 1959 a constitution was promulgated for Brunei and the arms—or crest, as it is known locally—was added to the flag. These arms are said to date back to the third sultan of Brunei, who ruled in the early 15th century.

The flag and umbrella are symbols of royalty. The wings have feathers ▶ P. 248

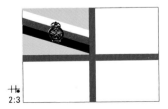
2:3

1:2   ROYAL FLAG

45

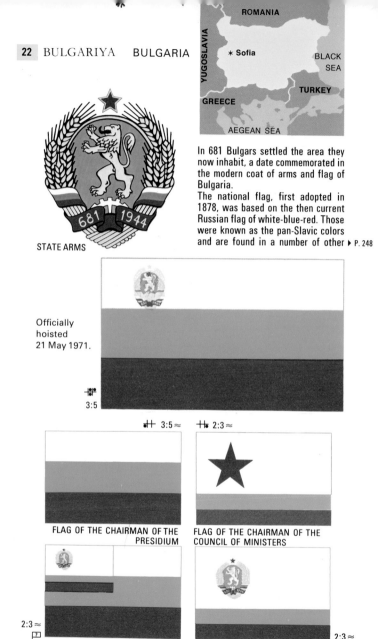

22 BULGARIYA BULGARIA

ROMANIA

YUGOSLAVIA

★ Sofia

BLACK SEA

GREECE

TURKEY

AEGEAN SEA

STATE ARMS

In 681 Bulgars settled the area they now inhabit, a date commemorated in the modern coat of arms and flag of Bulgaria.

The national flag, first adopted in 1878, was based on the then current Russian flag of white-blue-red. Those were known as the pan-Slavic colors and are found in a number of other ▶ P. 248

Officially hoisted 21 May 1971.

3:5

3:5 ≈ 2:3 ≈

FLAG OF THE CHAIRMAN OF THE PRESIDIUM

FLAG OF THE CHAIRMAN OF THE COUNCIL OF MINISTERS

2:3 ≈

2:3 ≈

The three stars in the flag and the three spears in the arms of Burundi are interpreted as symbols of the words in the national motto—"Unity, Work, Progress." However, they may also recall the three races that live in the nation—the Tutsi, Hutu, and Twa.

The colors of the Burundi flag are

STATE ARMS

Officially adopted 28 June 1967.

2:3 ≈

explained as symbolizing suffering and the struggle for independence (red), peace (white), and hope (green). The national flag is flown by the president and on public buildings, but its usage by private citizens is limited to certain holidays specified by law.

Formerly a sorghum plant, emblem of prosperity, and a royal drum were represented in the center of the flag. Because of their close association with the ruling dynasty, these symbols were removed following the republican revolution of 1966.

The vexillologist often finds a plausible or even likely condition which he cannot establish as factually correct because documentation is lacking.

For example, the diagonal cross in the flag of Burundi appears to have been inspired by the old flag of Sabena World Airlines, the Belgian national carrier; but no concrete proof of this exists.

CAPE VERDE

STATE ARMS

Two forms of livelihood predominate in the islands—farming and fishing. Corn, the chief local crop and staple food, well justifies—except in years of drought—the country's designation as a "green cape."

The seashell appearing in the national arms and flag symbolizes the insular and maritime nature of the

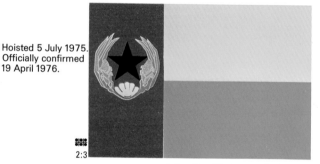

Hoisted 5 July 1975. Officially confirmed 19 April 1976.

2:3

state. The black star is for the independence of a black African state. The coat of arms also has a book for culture, a cogwheel for labor, and the national motto—"Unity, Labor, Progress."

Red in the flag symbolizes the blood of martyrs and heroes who brought the people, through armed struggle, to freedom and independence. Green proclaims the hope of the land and its tropical verdure. The well-being of the people, as well as the harvesting of the fruits of their labor, is represented by the yellow.

In part because many Cape Verdeans worked as civil servants and teachers in Portuguese Guinea under the colonial regime, close ties exist between Cape Verde and Guinea-Bissau. The countries have announced their intention eventually to unite and there are links between the ruling political parties. The sense of solidarity is expressed in graphic form through the similarity of the national arms and flags of the two countries.

STATE ARMS

As part of a program to increase national consciousness, a national flag was adopted in 1957 while Cameroon was still under French rule. Its vertical stripes were like those of the French Tricolor, but the colors were the pan-African green, red, and yellow. Cameroon was the second modern African nation (after Ghana)

Officially hoisted
20 May 1975

2:3 ≈

to adopt these colors, later copied by many other French-speaking African lands.

In 1961 the British territory of Southern Cameroons voted to join Cameroon. This was the basis for adding two gold stars to the Cameroon flag in that year. That flag symbolized the two cultures, British and French, united in one land.

The desire for national unity eventually resulted in the termination of the federal regime and creation of a unitary state in 1972. Three years later the flag was changed to reflect the political facts and the two stars were replaced by a single one emphasizing the unity of the Cameroonian people.

Green and yellow stand for the hope of a prosperous future and the sun. They also symbolize the forests in the south of Cameroon and the savannahs of its north, while red represents unity between them.

In the coat of arms the triangle bearing the map recalls Mount Cameroon, the highest point in West Africa. Also included is the national motto "Peace, Work, Fatherland."

49

STATE ARMS

The Colonial Naval Defense Act was adopted by the British parliament in 1865, two years before British colonies in North America entered into Confederation. Canada was authorized by that act to display on government vessels a "defaced" or modified British Blue Ensign. Although its usage was restricted, this—the first

1:2

Officially hoisted 15 February 1965.

ROYAL FLAG   8:13 ≈

GOVERNOR-GENERAL'S FLAG   1:2

Canadian "national flag"—became the basis for designs lasting almost a century.

The "seal" of Canada granted by Queen Victoria on 26 May 1868 was a shield quartered of the arms of Ontario, Quebec, Nova Scotia, and New Brunswick. This was represented in the fly of the Blue Ensign and, unofficially, on the British Red Ensign. In the latter—approved on 2 February 1892—the shield frequently was surrounded by a wreath of maple leaves, a beaver, and a royal crown. Unofficially, the shield often reflected the establishment of a new province by the addition of a local emblem. Merchant vessels, private citizens on land, and even public ▶ P. 2

929.9
SM67

BRITISH COLUMBIA
NEWFOUNDLAND
MANITOBA
ALBERTA
NEW BRUNSWICK
NOVA SCOTIA

1:2

ALBERTA
Officially hoisted 1 June 1968.

BRITISH COLUMBIA
Officially adopted 20 June 1960.

3:5 ≈

NEW BRUNSWICK/NOUVEAU-BRUNSWICK
Officially hoisted 25 March 1965.

1:2

MANITOBA
Officially hoisted 12 May 1966.

5:8

1:2

NEWFOUNDLAND
Officially adopted 15 May 1931.

NOVA SCOTIA
Officially confirmed 19 January 1929.

3:4 ≈

21,505

51

NORTHWEST TERRITORIES
THE YUKON

QUEBEC

SASKATCHEWAN
ONTARIO
PRINCE EDWARD ISLAND

🏴 1:2

ONTARIO
Officially hoisted 21 May 1965.

PRINCE EDWARD ISLAND
Officially hoisted 24 March 1964.

🏴 2:3

🏴 2:3

QUÉBEC/QUEBEC
Officially adopted 21 January 1948.

SASKATCHEWAN
Officially hoisted 22 September 1969.

🏴 1:2

🏴 1:2

THE YUKON
Officially adopted 1 March 1968.

NORTHWEST TERRITORIES
Officially adopted 31 January 1969.

🏴 1:2

STATE ARMS

In 1158, Holy Roman Emperor Frederick Barbarossa granted a coat of arms to Bohemia which is in use to this day—a white rampant lion with a double tail displayed on a field of red. The colors of this emblem became associated with agitation for Czech autonomy in the late nineteenth century when Bohemians and Moravians

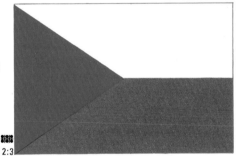

Officially adopted 30 March 1920; reestablished 1945.

2:3

PRESIDENTIAL FLAG

1:1

created a white-over-red bicolor. In 1918 this became the flag of the new Czechoslovak Republic.

Slovaks hoisted a horizontal tricolor in the revolution of 1848 whose white-blue-red colors were recognized as symbolizing pan-Slavic nationalism. In 1920 a blue triangle was introduced into the Czechoslovak flag to stand for Slovakia—an especially appropriate symbol since the new Slovak arms featured in blue the traditional mountains Tatra, Matra, and Fatra.

The presidential flag includes linden leaves and the motto "Truth Conquers."

The national epic of Chile, *La Araucana*, is a 16th century saga of precolonial life by Alonso de Ercilla. This tale of the Araucanian Indians speaks of warriors wearing sashes of white, blue, and red, although they had no flag.

Like other countries, Chile had many actual flags and proposed designs in

POR LA RAZON O LA FUERZA

STATE ARMS

Officially adopted ca. 18 October 1817.

2:3

PRESIDENTIAL FLAG

2:3

The supporters in the arms are the condor and the huemal, a deer that lives in the forests and high plateaus of the Andes. The national motto—"By Right or Might"—is emblazoned below the arms.

the early years of its struggle for independence. The design finally chosen was inspired by the Stars and Stripes of the United States. The Chilean flag has been used unchanged for over a century and a half, although during the 19th century the civil ensign omitted the star. The three colors of the flag are frequently met with in the flags of Chilean political parties.

The people of Chile generally see in the white stripe the snow of the Andes, which form the eastern border of their land. In the blue they see the sky and in the red, the blood of those who have died in defense of the country. The white star is a guide on the path of progress and honor.

STATE ARMS

The red color of the national flag is a symbol of Communism, but also has for centuries symbolized the Han (Chinese) people. Likewise the five stars have both a modern and ancient meaning. Chinese philosophical writings speak of the Five Rulers, Five Colors, Five Elements, Five Virtues, Five Classics, and so forth. The

Officially hoisted 1 October 1949.

2:3

2:3 ≈

Agriculture and industry are symbolized by the wheat and rice and by the cogwheel of the arms. The Gate of Heavenly Peace in Peking symbolizes restoration of power to the traditional Chinese capital.

country is composed of five parts—China Proper, Manchuria, Mongolia, Sinkiang, and Tibet. The five stars of the modern flag were conceived as symbolizing the leadership of the Communist party and its united front of workers, peasants, petty bourgeoisie, and patriotic capitalists.

The star in the flag of the People's Liberation Army (PLA) stands for its victories, won during the long struggle to expel foreign powers from China and unite the country. The date of foundation of the PLA is shown by stylized characters for "8" and "1" (for 1 August 1928) on its red banner.

STATE ARMS

On 16 March 1895 the political movement that eventually became the Kuomintang (Nationalist Party) adopted a flag designed by Lu Hao-tung. It is still in use as the party flag, as the jack of the Republic of China, and as a part of many other flags.

The sun is the essence of the *yang* or male principle which the Chinese hail as the positive force of universal existence associated with life, heaven, vigor, and pure and just administration in government. The twelve rays are seen as the spirit of unceasing progress throughout the twelve two-hour periods of the day.

On 1 September 1914 a red flag bearing the Kuomintang flag as its ▶ P.

Officially adopted
8 October 1928.

2:3

PRESIDENTIAL FLAG

2:3

2:3

8:11 ≈

CITTÀ DEL VATICANO
VATICAN CITY

STATE ARMS

Throughout the Middle Ages red was the color of the Catholic Church; gold was used for the crossed papal keys. In 1808 Napoleon amalgamated the pontifical army into his own and Pope Pius VII felt that new colors were needed. He chose yellow and white; in 1825 they were approved for various official flags of the Pontifical

Officially hoisted 8 June 1929.

1:1

State. Incorporated into Italy in 1870, this state was revived in 1929 as Vatican City and its flag was resurrected.

The tiara and crossed keys have been used as papal symbols since at least the 13th century. The latter are referred to in Matthew 16:19 and are traditionally associated with St. Peter.

PONTIFICAL ARMS

57

CARIBBEAN
SEA

PANAMA   VENEZUELA

PACIFIC   ★ Bogotá
OCEAN

ECUADOR   BRAZIL
        PERU

STATE ARMS

Although independence had been proclaimed three years before, it was not
until 1814 that a national flag was
established for Colombia. This, the
flag of the province of Cartagena
(already in use since 1811), had
concentric rectangles of red, yellow,
and green with a white eight-pointed
star in the center. In 1813

Officially adopted
26 November
1861.

2:3 ≈

Instead of the eagle frequent in
European heraldry, a number of
South American nations—
Colombia, Ecuador, Bolivia, and
Chile—have adopted the condor
as a distinctive national bird.
The old name of Colombia—New
Granada—is suggested by the
pomegranate *(granada* in
Spanish) at the top of its shield.
The wealth of the New World is
reflected in the cornucopias
which flank it. The other symbols
are a liberty cap and a represen-
tation of the isthmus separating
the Atlantic and Pacific.

Cundinamarca raised a flag of blue,
yellow, and red which is basically the
same flag it flies today as a province.
In 1819 the flag of Venezuela was
officially adopted for use by
Colombia; even after 1830, when
Colombia separated from Venezuela,
the flag was unchanged. The basic
design showed unequal horizontal
stripes of yellow (the top half of the
flag), blue, and red. Three blue stars
were sometimes added near the hoist
on the yellow to stand for Colombia,
Venezuela, and Ecuador. The colors
were said to be for the Colombian
people (yellow), the ocean separating
Colombia from Spain (blue), and the
blood (red) the people were willing to
shed in protecting themselves against

COLOMBIAN DEPARTMENTS

MAGDALENA

ANTIOQUIA

CUNDINAMARCA

HUILA

2:3

2:3

PRESIDENTIAL FLAG

3:5 ≈

any attempt by Spain to reimpose its will on Colombia.

In 1834, as the Republic of New Granada, Colombia adopted a flag of red-blue-yellow vertical stripes bearing the state arms for its war flag and ensign and state flag. The eight-pointed star replaced the arms in the civil ensign. The same design elements appeared in flags adopted in 1854, 1861 (when the stripes became horizontal again), 1886, 1890, 1934, 1949, and 1955. Most of these changes only involved new artistic renditions of the arms.

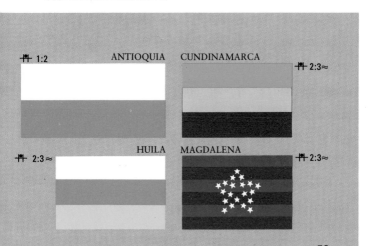

1:2   ANTIOQUIA   CUNDINAMARCA   2:3 ≈

2:3 ≈   HUILA   MAGDALENA   2:3 ≈

59

* Moroni

MOZAMBIQUE

MADAGASCAR

INDIAN OCEAN

The Islamic religion of the Comoro people is expressed by the green color and the crescent, long associated with Muslim tradition. The four stars are for the four islands of Grand Comoro, Mohéli, Anjouan, and Mayotte, although the last is not ruled by the Comoros.

The present flag is similar to the one

Officially adopted 1 October 1978.

3:5 ≈

In the 19th century Mayotte became a French colony and the island came to have a sizable Catholic population with a culture heavily influenced by France.

When the Comoros became independent, residents of Mayotte were concerned about their future under a Muslim majority less oriented toward European ways. A referendum supported the separation of that island from the other three. Thus today Mayotte remains a French territory, even though it is claimed by the Comoros and is represented in the national flag by a star.

adopted in 1963. In that design (by French heraldist Suzanne Gauthier) the stars stretched from the lower hoist to the upper fly of the flag and a (smaller) crescent appeared in the upper hoist with its horns facing the fly end of the flag. That flag continued to fly following the unilaterial proclamation of Comoro independence on 6 July 1975.

In November 1975 when the Comoros joined the United Nations, a new flag was adopted. It was composed of two unequal horizontal stripes, red over green. A crescent and four white stars arranged in a diamond pattern were set in the upper hoist. That flag was replaced by the current design, of more traditional symbolism, following a coup in 1978.

The Congo has no coat of arms.

In 1959 the Republic of the Congo adopted a flag of its own, although still linked to France by the Community. That flag had diagonal stripes of the pan-African colors— green, yellow, and red. No change was introduced when the Congo became independent on 15 August 1960.

Officially hoisted 30 December 1969.

2:3

In 1963 a socialist government was instituted and on the last day of 1969 a people's republic was proclaimed. To symbolize solidarity with other socialist countries, the flag was altered to the present design in which red predominates. That color is seen as a symbol of the Congolese people's struggle for national independence during the colonial era. The green palm branches stand for peace, and the gold star at the top is for hope. A hammer and hoe indicate the classes united in the building of a new Congo, workers and peasants.

The hoe of the native farmer has replaced the sickle as a symbol of agriculture in the adaptation of the Soviet symbol used by the Congo. Non-socialist African countries also make use of the hoe as a national symbol. Hoes are found in the arms of Upper Volta, Tanzania, The Gambia, Equatorial Guinea, Angola, Mozambique, Rwanda, Zambia, and the flags of the ruling political parties in Somalia and Tanzania.

NICARAGUA   CARIBBEAN SEA

★ San José   PANAMA

PACIFIC OCEAN

STATE ARMS

Alone among the former members of the United Provinces of the Center of America, Costa Rica decided that it was improper to continue to use the flag of that federation following its dissolution. At first a flag of white-blue-white was adopted, but in 1848 the five stripes still found in the national flag were selected.

Officially adopted 21 October 1964.

3:5

2:3 ≈

While the law allows private citizens only to decorate their homes with pennants in the national colors on holidays, in practice the civil ensign is also flown as a civil flag in Costa Rica

Blue and white recall the former flag of the Central American federation, as do the volcanoes in the coat of arms. The red was added in tribute to the French Revolution of 1848. Since that time the arms of Costa Rica have twice been modified slightly.

At present the arms bear the name of the country and at the top "Central America," a reminder of past unity and an expression of the hope that Costa Rica may again in the future be part of a larger state. The stars correspond to the number of provinces in Costa Rica.

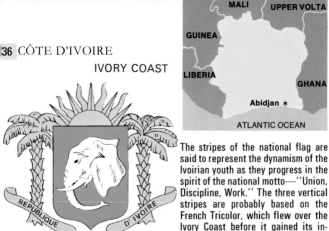

36 CÔTE D'IVOIRE

IVORY COAST

STATE ARMS

The stripes of the national flag are said to represent the dynamism of the Ivoirian youth as they progress in the spirit of the national motto—"Union, Discipline, Work." The three vertical stripes are probably based on the French Tricolor, which flew over the Ivory Coast before it gained its independence in 1960.

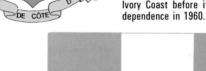

Officially adopted
3 December 1959.

2:3

Originally the shield in the national arms was blue, but in 1964 a new decree altered the color to green to conform more closely with the national flag. The elephant, which figures as the principal charge of the shield, is not only an indigenous beast but also the party emblem of the Ivory Coast Democratic Party that led the country to independence. The "white gold" of the elephant, which attracted early European traders and conquerors, gave the nation its distinctive name.

The savannas of the north are recalled in the orange stripe, while the green is an expression of the virgin forests of the southern regions. White symbolically stands for unity between north and south. The same general symbolism is found in the orange-white-green flag of Niger.
Orange, white, and green have also been interpreted to mean respectively: the spirit of national development, peace and purity, and hope for the future through the utilization of natural resources.

STATE ARMS

When Narciso López designed the Cuban flag, the first one was sewn by Emilia Teurbe Tolón. Her husband, Miguel, created the Cuban coat of arms by combining traditional symbols of republicanism—the liberty cap and fasces—with distinctive Cuban emblems. The position of Cuba as the key to the Gulf of Mexico, for

1:2

Officially hoisted 20 May 1902.

PRESIDENTIAL FLAG

1:1

The national flag and coat of arms were developed by exiled Cubans in New York in the mid-19th century and, in part, derived their inspiration from the United States flag.

example, is represented in the chief of the shield.

Both the flag and arms have three blue stripes to correspond to the territorial subdivisions of Cuba at the time the flag was created. The white stripes are for the purity of the revolutionary cause.

The star of independence is set on a triangle, the Masonic symbol of liberty and equality. Red suggests the bloody struggles the nation faced in achieving and preserving independence. The Cuban flag served as the model for the flag of neighboring Puerto Rico.

STATE ARMS

A famous story known to every schoolchild in Denmark relates that the Dannebrog fell from heaven on 15 June 1219, during a battle in which King Waldemar II was victorious against the pagan Estonians. Another source traces its origin to a battle in 1208. More recent scholarship indicates that the likely origin of the ▶ P. 249

In use since the 13th or 14th century; officially confirmed 1625.

28:37

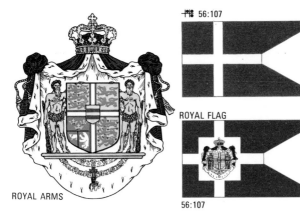

ROYAL ARMS

56:107

ROYAL FLAG

56:107

65

STATE ARMS

When the constitution of the Federal Republic of Germany was being written in 1949, its authors naturally rejected the flags of black, red, and white which had characterized the Nazi Third Reich and the Second Reich (1871–1919). On the other hand the Federal Republic also rejected any entirely new design, although

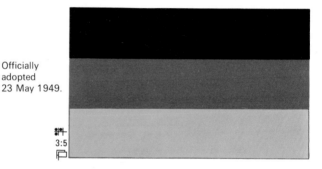

Officially adopted 23 May 1949.

3:5

PRESIDENTIAL FLAG

1:1

many proposals for such flags were submitted at the time. Instead Germans turned to the black-red-gold flag which had been official from 1919 to 1933.

That flag had originated in the early 19th century when Germany was divided into dozens of independent and semi-independent states. The colors ▶ P.

3:5

3:5

HAMBURG
BREMEN
BERLIN
HESSE
BAVARIA
BADEN-WÜRTTEMBERG

▼ LAND BADEN-WÜRTTEMBERG

3:5

STATE OF BADEN-WURTTEMBERG
Off. adopted 29 September 1954.

FREISTAAT BAYERN ▼
FREE STATE OF BAVARIA
Officially adopted
14 December 1953.

3:5 ≈

▲ LAND BERLIN
STATE OF BERLIN
Officially adopted 26 May 1954.

FREIE HANSESTADT BREMEN ▼
FREE HANSEATIC CITY OF BREMEN
Off. confirmed 21 November 1947.

15:23 ≈

2:3 ≈

LAND HESSEN ▼
STATE OF HESSE
Off. adopted 31 December 1949.

▲ FREIE UND HANSESTADT HAMBURG
FREE AND HANSEATIC CITY OF HAMBURG
Usage initiated 8 October 1897.

3:5

67

SCHLESWIG-HOLSTEIN ——

LOWER SAXONY ——

NORTH RHINE-WESTPHALIA ——

RHINELAND-PALATINATE ——
THE SAAR ——

2:3

▲ LAND NIEDERSACHSEN
STATE OF LOWER SAXONY

Officially adopted 17 October 1952.

2:3

▲ LAND RHEINLAND-PFALZ
STATE OF RHINELAND-PALATINATE
Officially adopted 15 May 1948.

3:5

LAND SCHLESWIG-HOLSTEIN ▲
STATE OF SCHLESWIG HOLSTEIN
Officially adopted 18 January 1957.

LAND NORDRHEIN-WESTFALEN ▾
STATE OF NORTH RHINE-WESTPHALIA
Officially adopted 10 March 1953.

3:5

SAARLAND ▾
SAAR STATE
Off. adopted 10 September 1956.

3:5

Most flags in Germany are composed of heraldic colors, with or without a representation of the arms in addition. Although adopted in their present forms only recently, many of the German state flags go back hundreds of years to an era when they represented separate powers with fortresses and warships of their own.

GERMANY

STATE ARMS

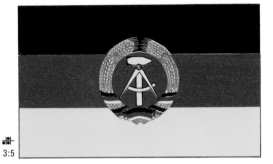

The German Democratic Republic (GDR) during the first ten years of its existence flew the traditional black-red-gold German colors. To distinguish this flag from that of the Federal Republic of Germany, the state arms were added in 1959 to various GDR flags.

The elements in these arms express

Officially hoisted 1 October 1959.

3:5

3:5

the ideological orientation of the state. Red shows its commitment to Communism; the tricolored ribbon reflects the national character of the state. Peasants, manual laborers, and intellectuals are represented by the wheat, hammer, and pair of dividers.

3:5

CHAIRMAN OF THE STATE COUNCIL FLAG

1:1

41 DIVEHI   MALDIVES

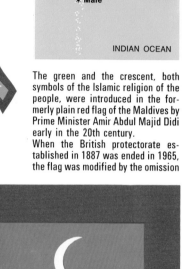

ARABIAN SEA   **INDIA**

SRI LANKA

★ **Male**

INDIAN OCEAN

STATE ARMS

The green and the crescent, both symbols of the Islamic religion of the people, were introduced in the formerly plain red flag of the Maldives by Prime Minister Amir Abdul Majid Didi early in the 20th century.

When the British protectorate established in 1887 was ended in 1965, the flag was modified by the omission

Officially hoisted 26 July 1965.

2:3

of the black and white diagonally striped border which had appeared along the hoist.

The national arms feature a date palm, national flags, and a star and crescent above the name of the state on a scroll.

2:3

PRESIDENTIAL FLAG

⊹ 3:5≈

3:5≈

PRIME MINISTER'S FLAG

70

STATE ARMS

From 1832 to 1847 Abd el-Kader led resistance forces struggling to keep Algeria free from French military occupation. Their eventual defeat led to more than a century of French colonial power in Algeria. Today Abd el-Kader is honored by an independent Algeria. He is popularly credited with having created the design which

Officially hoisted 3 July 1962.

2:3

The crescent and star motif has been a common symbol of Islamic culture in North Africa for centuries, particularly under the Ottoman rule which preceded French conquests. Green is also recognized as a traditional Muslim color.

The Arabic letter *djim* appears twice on the state arms as an abbreviation for the former long-form name of the country, Algerian Republic. These arms, although official, are rarely used.

is now the national flag, although this has not been substantiated. It appears more likely that the flag was designed by Messali Hadj in 1928. His North Africa Star, founded two years before, was the first serious effort to organize Algerian Muslims politically. Even though the Front of National Liberation (FLN) adopted Messali Hadj's flag in 1954, its own radical program and revolutionary tactics came to dominate the independence struggle. Following the establishment of the Provisional Government of the Algerian Republic in 1958 by the FLN, the flag became known throughout the world.

STATE ARMS

The national motto of Djibouti—"Unity, Equality, Peace"—may be seen reflected in the design of its national flag. White is a traditional color for peace and the five-pointed star has been used by many nations as a symbol for unity. (Others have seen the red star as signifying the struggle for independence.) The triangle is an

21:38 ≈

Officially hoisted 27 June 1977.

ideal emblem for equality.

The flag had been used since 1972 by the People's African League for Independence, which led the movement to end French colonialism in what was then known as the Territory of the Afars and Issas. The green stripe in its flag stood for the Afars, referring both to their land and Muslim faith. The light blue stripe was associated with the Issas. Although also of the Islamic faith, the Issas are related to the people of neighboring Somalia, whose colors are blue and white. At the time of independence the president of Djibouti stated that blue was a symbol of the sea and sky and that green stood for the earth.

Heraldic purists of Europe still insist that a proper coat of arms must consist of a design on a shield. This may be decorated by optional accessories such as crest, supporters, motto. In actual usage those accessories are inalienable parts of modern national coats of arms and a shield is often completely missing—as in the arms of Djibouti. Function not form—i.e., modes of usage rather than the appearance of a design—defines the modern national coat of arms.

ATLANTIC OCEAN

DOMINICAN REPUBLIC

Roseau ✳

CARIBBEAN SEA

STATE ARMS

Officially hoisted 3 November 1978.

The Catholic faith of Dominica is reflected in the cross of the flag and the somewhat similar one in the national coat of arms. The three colors of the former are specifically associated with the Christian trinity. Stars for each of Dominica's parishes ring a central red disk, seen as a token of the socialist program for

1:2

PRESIDENTIAL FLAG   1:2

In the mountainous regions of the island live many rare species of parrots. To honor the *sisserou* or imperial parrot, a representation of that bird was included on either side of the shield of arms established in 1961. Its motto means "After the Good Lord [we love] the Earth."

development which Dominica has adopted. The national bird is "an emblem of flight toward greater heights and fulfillment of aspirations."

The colors of the design refer both to the land and the people. Yellow is for citrus fruits and bananas, as well as for the Carib Indians who live in the northeast. The rich black soil of Dominica and the people of African descent whose labor makes it fruitful are expressed in the black arms of the cross. White refers to the purity of aspirations of the people and the pure rivers and waterfalls which abound on Dominica. The rich vegetation which covers the island recommended the principal national color, green.

73

ROYAL ARMS

P.R. CHINA

★ Thimphu

INDIA

The yellow or saffron half of the flag is symbolic of the authority of the king and signifies his active role in directing religious and secular affairs. The lower half of the flag symbolizes the spiritual power of Buddhism, represented in Bhutan by the Kagyudpa and Nyingmapa sects. This color formerly was maroon, but was altered in

Usage initiated in the nineteenth century.

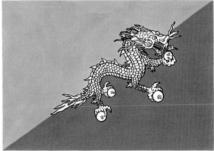

2:3

the 1960s to orange-red. White is seen as an emblem of both loyalty and purity.

The dragon in the center has several symbolic functions. It refers to the name of the country, which translates as "Land of the Dragon." It also refers to thunder, often heard in the valleys and mountains of Bhutan and traditionally believed to be the voice of dragons. In the past Bhutan had close relations with the emperors of China whose flag was golden yellow with a dragon.

In the center of the royal arms is a stylized thunderbolt, associated with the power of the lamas. The head of a monastery, for example, is known as *Dorjéraja* or Wielder of the Thunderbolt. It is seen today as an emblem of power and authority as well as of harmony between spiritual and secular laws. At the top of the royal arms is the triple gem of Buddhist philosophy, which also appeared in the 1912–1959 flag of Tibet.

STATE ARMS

GALAPAGOS IS. ★ Quito

PACIFIC OCEAN   PERU

In the first years of its independence, Ecuador was part of a union comprising Colombia and Venezuela. The national flag it hoisted in 1830 when the federation was dissolved retained the same basic design as the federation flag.

As in many other South American countries, private citizens fly a flag of

1:2

In use since 1860; officially adopted 7 November 1900.

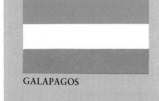

GALAPAGOS

plain stripes while national government buildings and military installations add the national coat of arms. Ecuador is unique, however, in having a special flag for use on municipal buildings with a ring of stars, one for each of the provinces. The arms include "that portion of the Zodiac which contains the signs corresponding to the memorable months of March, April, May and June," recalling the revolution that took place during those months in 1845. It also shows Mount Chimborazo and a ship that stands for navigation and trade.

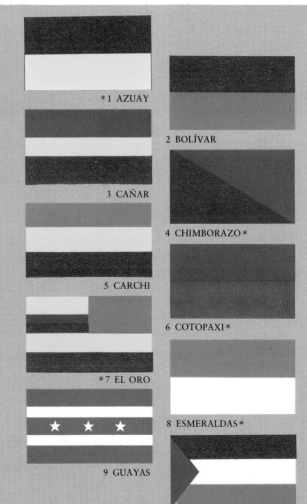

*1 AZUAY

2 BOLÍVAR

3 CAÑAR

4 CHIMBORAZO*

5 CARCHI

6 COTOPAXI*

*7 EL ORO

8 ESMERALDAS*

9 GUAYAS

10 IMBABURA

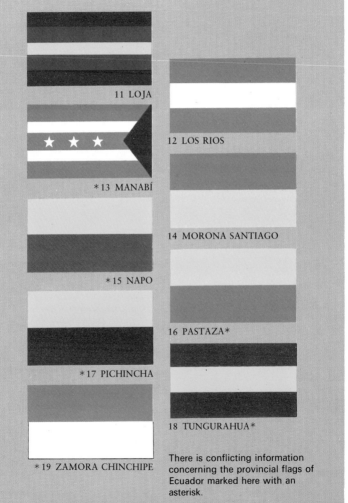

11 LOJA

12 LOS RIOS

*13 MANABÍ

14 MORONA SANTIAGO

*15 NAPO

16 PASTAZA*

*17 PICHINCHA

18 TUNGURAHUA*

*19 ZAMORA CHINCHIPE

There is conflicting information
concerning the provincial flags of
Ecuador marked here with an
asterisk.

STATE ARMS

The harp has been an Irish national symbol since at least the 15th century. The Brian Boru harp (today at Trinity College in Dublin) is the model for the modern representation of the arms, but variations have existed in the past. The traditional green Irish flag with the golden harp was based on the arms of the province of

1:2

Official confirmed 29 December 1937.

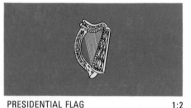

PRESIDENTIAL FLAG   1:2

Leinster.

Green figured in almost all flags raised by the Catholic majority as they struggled to end English rule over their land. Irish Protestants, recalling the victory of King William III in the Battle of the Boyne in 1690, have used his livery color (orange) since that time.

In the 19th century, under the influence of France, the Irish revolutionary movement began to fly a tricolor which included a white stripe for peace. It has been used in Ireland since independence was proclaimed on 21 January 1919.

1:2   CONNDAE CILLE MANNTAIN
WICKLOW COUNTY

STATE ARMS

For many years El Salvador flew a flag of stars and stripes based on that of the United States, but in 1912 the blue-white-blue flag of its early days of independence was reestablished. This flag is considered a symbol of solidarity with the other Central American nations.

The most recent flag law in El

Officially hoisted ca. 27 September 1972.

3:5

189:335

Salvador recognizes three official versions of the same basic design. One features the national motto—"God, Union, Liberty." Another includes this motto as part of the coat of arms. The Masonic triangle of liberty and equality in the arms is framed by a wreath whose fourteen clusters of leaves correspond to the number of departments in El Salvador. The triangle contains a liberty cap, five volcanoes between two oceans, a rainbow, and the independence date "15 September 1821."

3:5

STATE ARMS

"A Man is a Man": the motto at the top of the state arms affirms a belief in the equality of all people, as graphically expressed in the national flag. The blue, white, and red of the French flag (which flew during the colonial regime) and the green, yellow, and red pan-African colors are united to show that Europeans and

Officially
hoisted
1 December
1958.

3:5 ≈

2:3 ≈   IMPERIAL FLAG

The imperial standard of Bokassa I combines the favorite color (green) and emblem (the eagle) of Napoleon I of France with the sun which serves as a crest in the national arms. Transformation of the Central African Republic into an empire did not affect its national flag.

Africans must have respect and friendship for one another. Their common bond—the red blood of humanity—forms the vertical stripe in the Central African flag.

Green and yellow have been given specific meanings, the former representing the people of the forest region and the latter those of the savannah. The gold star of independence is a guide toward future progress.

The coat of arms includes the Central African Order of Merit, the national motto ("Unity, Dignity, Work"), and the date of proclamation of the empire. The star and map indicate the location of the country.

STATE ARMS

The central shield in the national arms indicates the source of red and yellow in the national flag of Spain—the arms of Castile, Leon, Aragon, and Navarre. The basic red-yellow-red Spanish flag dates from a royal decree of 28 May 1785. The first record of a lion as a symbol of Leon seems to be found on coins issued

Officially adopted 29 August 1936.

2:3

2:3

under Alfonso VII (1126–1157); Alfonso VIII introduced the castle of Castile on his coins. A century later under Ferdinand III the two were combined in a quartered fashion, exactly as they are to be seen in the first and fourth quarters of the Spanish arms today.

▶ P. 250

PRIME MINISTER'S FLAG

ROYAL FLAG

1:1   1:1

ASTURIAS
BASQUE PROVINCES
ARAGON
ANDALUSIA
CANARY ISLANDS

웨 2:3

ANDALUCÍA
ANDALUSIA

ARAGON 웨 2:3

웨 2:3 ASTURIAS

PAÍS VASCO 웨 2:3
BASQUE PROVINCES

웨 2:3 CANARIAS
CANARY ISLANDS

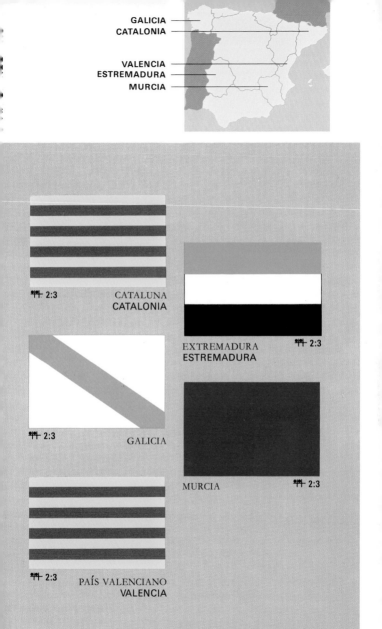

GALICIA
CATALONIA

VALENCIA
ESTREMADURA
MURCIA

2:3   CATALUNA
CATALONIA

EXTREMADURA
ESTREMADURA   2:3

2:3   GALICIA

MURCIA   2:3

2:3   PAÍS VALENCIANO
VALENCIA

RED
SEA

SUDAN   YEMEN

GULF OF ADEN

★ Addis   SOMALIA
Ababa

STATE ARMS

Prior to the overthrow of the ancient Ethiopian empire in 1974, red was seen as the color of strength, the blood of patriots, or faith. Yellow was for the church, peace, natural wealth, or love. Green was seen as a symbol of the land or of hope. Others related the colors to the Christian trinity or the three most important Ethiopian

Usage reestablished ca. 5 May 1941.

2:3

Designed in 1975 by Taddesse Mesfin, the Ethiopian arms feature a traditional plow in the center to emphasize the importance of agriculture. A cogwheel of 14 cogs suggests both industry and the 14 administrative districts of the country. National defense is stressed by the representation of a spear, sword, and shield.

Attached to the plow is a sling in the shape of the first letter of the Amharic alphabet; this emphasizes the need for education. Framing the shield are branches of the yellowwood and wild olive.

provinces.

Historically, the national flag may be dated to the late 19th century. At that time Ethiopia was struggling to preserve its national independence against imperialist incursions by Europeans. Although the French and Italians were unsuccessful in their attempts to control the country, their tricolored flags may have inspired the Ethiopian national flag.

First displayed as three separate pennants, the national flag was established in rectangular form on 6 October 1897. The red stripe was on the top and the ancient lion emblem of the emperor was represented in the center of the flag. The lion continues to figure in the national coat of arms.

STATE ARMS

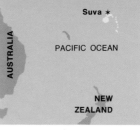

Suva *

PACIFIC OCEAN

NEW ZEALAND

The light blue field of the national flag was specifically chosen to distinguish it from the somewhat similar national flags of Australia and New Zealand. Blue was the most popular color in a competition held prior to independence to select a new flag. Under British rule, the government vessels from Fiji flew the British Blue ▶ P. 250

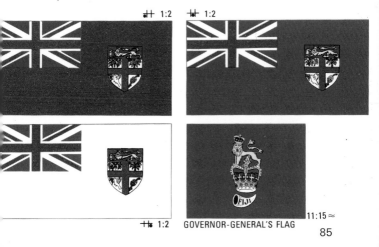

1:2

Officially hoisted 10 October 1970.

⊹ 1:2   ⊹ 1:2

⊹ 1:2   GOVERNOR-GENERAL'S FLAG   11:15 ≈

85

53 FØROYAR/FÆRØERNE
FAROES

ICELAND

NORWAY

★ Torshavn

ATLANTIC OCEAN

UNITED KINGDOM

STATE ARMS

Two students—Jens Oliver Lisberg and Janus Øssursson—were responsible for the design of the Faroes flag. They explained the symbolism as follows: "Its white color was to recall to all of us the foam of the sea and the clean, bright sky of the Faroe Islands, while the red and blue cross composed of the ancient Faroese colors

Officially adopted 5 June 1959.

8:11

would remind us of our tie to the other Nordic countries."

The flag was first flown in the islands on 22 June 1919 and was recognized in 1931 by the local parliament despite opposition by the Danish authorities.

After the war the king assented to the Home Rule Act on 23 March 1948, which allowed for the flying of the Faroese flag on ships and on land without restrictions.

The navy blue of the first official design was altered to azure blue 11 years later. Danish authorities in the Faroes continue to fly the state flag of Denmark.

Since the 14th century the Faroe Islands has had a representation of a ram in its seal and coat of arms. There is an old saying that "Sheep's wool is Faroes' gold." In the 19th century various proposed flags for the islands incorporated a ram—or an oyster catcher, the national bird.

The Faroe Islands is still a part of the Danish realm and has a quartering in the royal arms of Denmark which shows the ram.

There is no official coat of arms for the French Republic.

On 13 July 1789 when the Paris Militia was organized, the troops wore a cockade of the municipal colors, blue and red. Four days later the same revolutionary symbol was presented by the Marquis de Lafayette to the king, who wore it and his own white cockade when he greeted the crowd outside the City

Officially hoisted 20 May 1794; most recently reestablished 5 March 1848.

2:3

2:3

Hall. These three colors were officially adopted on 4 October 1789 as the French cockade—at that time a more important form of political symbol than the flag.

Red and blue had been used at least as early as 1358 by Parisian commoners revolting against royal authority. White had been introduced as ▶ P. 251

PRESIDENT'S FLAG   PRIME MINISTER'S FLAG

27:38/7:9 ≈   15:19 ≈

STATE ARMS

Officially adopted
9 August 1960.

3:4

Forests—whose lumber is a major contribution to the national economy—inspired the green stripe of the Gabon flag. An okumé tree displays and protects the shield of the national arms.

The blue and gold stripes emphasize that Gabon is a maritime nation through which the equator runs. Prior to independence the gold stripe was narrower than the other two, and the Tricolor of France, colonial master of Gabon, appeared as a canton.

The ship in the arms indicates an African nation traveling toward the brilliant future promised by its mineral wealth, as indicated by the gold disks at the top of the shield. In heraldry such disks are known as bezants, recalling the gold coins of the Byzantine Empire.

Two mottoes figure in the Gabon arms: the Latin translates as "United We Progress." The French slogan below proclaims "Union, Work, Justice."

PRESIDENTIAL FLAG

1:1

The shield of the arms—which serves as an armorial banner for the president—has black panthers as supporters. They were chosen to symbolize the vigilance and courage of the president who protects the nation.

STATE ARMS

The blue stripe running through the center of the flag represents the Gambia River, which flows through the center of the country. The agricultural resources of The Gambia and the sun are symbolized by the green and red stripes; white stands for unity and peace.

In the coat of arms the blue, white,

Officially hoisted 18 February 1965.

2:3

It is a British Commonwealth tradition for the sovereign to grant a flag and coat of arms to a colony (such as The Gambia) upon its independence. An official painting of each is prepared by the College of Arms in London and signed by the British monarch.

The grant becomes effective on independence day; often no law is promulgated to which reference can be made for exact details of the flag design. In other countries the national flag is usually defined by a law or even by the constitution.

and green are given slightly different interpretations. The first is said to stand for love and loyalty; the white is for the law-abiding nature of the Gambian people and their friendliness. In addition to agricultural resources, green reflects hope and broad-mindedness.

The agricultural implements—an axe and hoe—are seen as indications that the future prosperity of The Gambia depends upon the agricultural pursuits of its people. The lions are said to represent stateliness and dignity, but may also recall the British colonial regime that existed prior to independence.

STATE ARMS

The green-white-red horizontal tricolor of the ruling Convention People's Party and the green-yellow-red of Africa's oldest independent nation (Ethiopia) combined to inspire Ghana's flag. The black star is considered the lodestar of African freedom. Many other African countries have since adopted the colors of

Officially hoisted 6 March 1957; reestablished 28 February 1966.

2:3

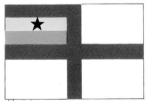

PRESIDENTIAL FLAG   7:12 ≈

this flag.

Symbols of local authority, the national economy, and Ghanaian history combine in a coat of arms of traditional Western pattern. In contrast, the emblem on the presidential flag is composed of authentic Ghanaian symbols meaning sovereignty, good luck, and sanctity.

2:3

2:3

90

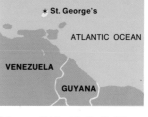

★ St. George's

ATLANTIC OCEAN

VENEZUELA

GUYANA

STATE ARMS

Only a small island in the Caribbean, Grenada is the world's second largest producer of nutmeg—hence, the representation of a nutmeg in the hoist triangle of the flag. The country is divided into seven parishes, each represented by a star in the flag— St. George, St. John, St. Mark, St. Patrick, St. Andrew, St. David, and

Officially
hoisted
7 February
1974.

3:5

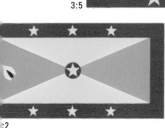

:2

In keeping with British Commonwealth practice, there are two versions of the same basic flag, differing in proportions when used at sea or on land.

the Grenadines. These parishes are also represented by the seven roses in the crest of the coat of arms. The colors which figure in both the flags and coat of arms have the following symbolism. Yellow stands for the sun and the friendliness of the Grenadian people. Green represents the agricultural basis of Grenada's economy, while red is for harmony, unity, and courage. The ship and lilies in the coat of arms recall that Grenada was discovered by Columbus and has been Catholic for centuries.

STATE ARMS

Centuries ago the Aztec and the Maya-Quiche civilizations of Central America had gods in the form of feathered serpents (Quetzalcohuatl and Gugunatz). In artwork, the serpents' feathers would be represented by the brilliant green plumes of the quetzal.

Today the national bird of Guatemala,

Officially
adopted
15 September
1968.

⌗+
5:8

⊞ 5:8

Although Guatemala was the capital of the United Provinces of the Center of America when independence was proclaimed in 1823, its symbols least resemble those of the original state among the five nations once united in that federation.

the quetzal is considered a symbol of liberty because it supposedly cannot live in captivity. General Justo Rufino Barrios introduced it as a national emblem in 1871, although the quetzal had been used decades earlier in the arms of the secessionist state of Los Altos.

Guatemala's arms bear a parchment scroll inscribed "Liberty 15 September 1821" in honor of the date when Central America broke with Spain. Like other former members of the United Provinces of the Center of America, Guatemala still uses a flag of blue, white, and blue.

EQUATORIAL GUINEA

STATE ARMS

The sole element retained by Equatorial Guinea from its original arms is the ribbon with the national motto—"Unity, Peace, Justice" (in Spanish).

The word "Labor" appearing in the new arms is exemplified by the tools, reminding the people of the necessity of self-reliance and hard work in the

Hoisted 1978.

5:8 ≈

Since earliest recorded history, men and women have chosen emblems to represent their religious and social organizations. The attributes of such symbols—the freedom of the eagle and the strength of the lion—have been qualities they saw in themselves or hoped for.

While other types of symbols have become more prominent in the past 200 years, forms of plant and animal life are still extremely common in national coats of arms. The cock used by Equatorial Guinea, for example, has also been a symbol in France, Ghana, Nigeria, Angola, Kenya, Alabama, and Belgium.

process of transforming the national economy. The hoe of the common farmer, found in several other African flags and arms, is crossed with a lumberman's axe. The other tools are a hoe, a pickaxe, a machete, and a file used for sharpening the latter tool. Above these stands a red cock, personal emblem of Francisco Macias Nguema, president for life of Equatorial Guinea. It calls on the people to awake and arise.

The flag has been used since independence on 12 October 1968, only the arms in the center having been altered. The green stripe represents the natural resources of the land; blue is for the water linking the mainland and the islands. White is for peace and red, the independence struggle.

93

STATE ARMS

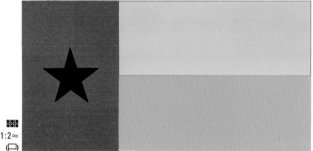

1:2≈

Officially hoisted 24 September 1973.

The African Party for the Independence of Guinea and Cape Verde (PAIGC) in August 1961 adopted black and the pan-African colors—red, yellow, and green—for its flag. Years of armed struggle eventually liberated most of (Portuguese) Guinea from colonialist rule. In 1973 independence was pro-

The emblem of the African Party for the Independence of Guinea and Cape Verde was transformed into the national coat of arms of Guinea-Bissau following independence. The common features of the two are palm leaves, a shell, and a star. The shell was for the Cape Verde Islands, the palm branches for Guinea-Bissau. The emblem bore a torch, signifying the struggle for liberty, and the motto "Unity and Struggle" in Portuguese. The national motto is an adaptation of this—"Unity, Struggle, Progress."

claimed under a national flag exactly like the PAIGC flag, except that the party initials were omitted from beneath the star. That star is seen as a symbol of Africa and its black people—their dignity, freedom, and peace.

The red stripe marks the work and struggle of the people, the suffering which they underwent in the colonial period, and the war needed to end it. Yellow is for the fruits of work, the harvest which assures the well-being of those who labor. Green is an emblem of the tropical nature of the country, as well as of hope for the future. The basic pattern of stripes in the flag is also found in the flag of Cape Verde, indicating the intention of the two countries to unite.

94

STATE ARMS

The flag chosen following Guinea's proclamation of independence in 1958 reflected its years under French rule by the three vertical stripes. The flag colors are those of the organization that led the struggle for independence, the Democratic Party of Guinea. These also correspond to the pan-African colors previously adopted

Officially adopted
10 November
1958.

2:3≈

PRESIDENTIAL FLAG

2:3

by Ethiopia, Ghana, and Cameroon. Finally, the colors are seen as a reflection of the national motto ''Work, Justice, Solidarity.'' Red is for the sweat running across the black bodies of the Guinean men and women who struggle to build their country and for the blood of patriotic martyrs. The golden sun which shines equally on all men suggests an identification of yellow with justice, although it is also an emblem of mineral wealth. The green of Guinea's vegetation evokes a spirit of solidarity among all citizens in the development of the national economy.

The commitment of Guinea's foreign policy to peace is symbolized by the dove and olive branch; the elephant is an emblem of strength used by the Democratic Party of Guinea.

95

STATE ARMS

"The Golden Arrowhead," as it is known to the Guyanese press, represents the golden future citizens hope will be built upon Guyana's mineral resources. The extensive water resources of the country are incorporated in the design through a white fimbriation that separates the arrowhead from the green field.

Officially hoisted 26 May 1966.

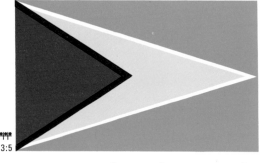

3:5

1:2

Green was chosen as an appropriate color for the flag background because green forests and fields cover more than 90 percent of Guyana.

Red is for zeal and sacrifice, elements of the dynamic nation-building process the Guyanese are engaged in. The black triangle border indicates the perseverance needed to achieve success in the undertaking. The author of this book designed Guyana's national flag.

Local attributes incorporated into the arms include a cacique's crown, diamonds, jaguars, agricultural products (sugar cane and rice), a pickaxe, and the national motto.

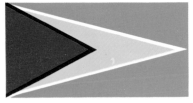

1:1 ≈

PRESIDENTIAL FLAG

STATE ARMS

The concepts of liberty, democracy, and the natural rights of man proclaimed by the French Revolution led the French colony of Saint-Domingue to proclaim its independence on 1 January 1804 as the Republic of Haiti.

Its first flag consisted of blue and red stripes symbolizing blacks and mulat-

🏴 ✚
1:2 ≈

Officially hoisted 21 June 1964.

:2 ≈ 🏳

A panoply of weapons has served as the Haitian national arms for over a century. The motto is the same as that of Belgium—"Union Makes Strength."

toes. The design omitted from the French Tricolor its central stripe, which Haitians saw as a symbol of the white slave holders.

Under Jean-Jacques Dessalines and Henri Christophe the blue was changed to black, but President Jean-Paul Boyer in 1822 established a horizontal blue-red flag which continued in use until 1964. At that time President François Duvalier brought back the early vertical black-red to stress links with Haiti's African heritage. Duvalier also removed the liberty cap above the emperor palm tree in the national arms, claiming that the latter was sufficient as a symbol of liberty.

STATE ARMS

The upper reaches of the Red Volta, the White Volta, and the Black Volta flow through this land. They provided the country with its name and the inspiration for its national flag. Simple horizontal stripes corresponding to the names of the three rivers are repeated in the national flag, the national coat of arms, and the pres-

Officially
adopted
9 December
1959.

2:3

PRESIDENTIAL FLAG

1:1

idential standard.

The coat of arms, adopted in 1961, has two further charges indirectly related to the rivers. The water they provide is used to raise sorghum; consequently, this plant and the hoes used in its cultivation figure at the bottom of the arms. An appropriate symbol for an agricultural people, a hoe may also be found in the flag of the Congo and in the arms of Zambia, Tanzania, Rwanda, The Gambia, and Liberia.

The use of three-word national mottoes—such as Upper Volta's "Unity, Labor, Justice"—characterizes many countries, especially those which have at some time been under French rule.

66 HELLAS   GREECE

STATE ARMS

Officially
hoisted
March 1822;
reestablished
22 December
1978.

2:3

Adoption of a definitive national flag—the same design in use today—took place following the proclamation of Greek independence on 13 January 1822. The flag was stated to symbolize "the wisdom of God, freedom, and country." The blue is generally seen as a reminder of the sea and sky, white indicating the purity of the independence struggle. The cross in the canton is a reminder of Greek religious faith, while the nine stripes of the flag correspond to the nine syllables in the war cry of independence: "Freedom or Death." The shade of blue has varied over the years, sometimes unofficially and sometimes to indicate political and dynastic associations. For example, in the 19th century the Greek royal dynasty was of Bavarian origin and a medium blue was employed. The military junta which ruled Greece from 1967 to 1974 insisted on a very dark blue, while the latest flag law speaks of "light blue" without giving any scientific definition to the term.

Greece has frequently used a flag of blue with a white cross extending to the four edges of the flag. That flag was flown on land by private citizens (except in seaports) until abolished in 1970. Reinstated in 1975 as the sole official flag for all purposes, in practice it was not used on ships, which continued to display the striped flag. The latest flag law reverts to the situation of 1970–1975, the striped flag being official for all purposes on land and at sea.

HELVETIA/
SCHWEIZ/
SUISSE/
SVIZZERA/
SVIZZRA
SWITZERLAND

Emblazoned in white on the Blood Banner of the Holy Roman Empire, the Swiss cross appeared on battlefields wherever Swiss soldiers fought in the name of the confederation. While the similar emblem of the canton of Schwyz dates from 1240, for the confederation itself our first written record is more recent: troops leaving

STATE ARMS

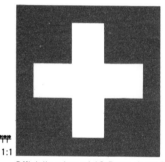

1:1

Officially adopted 12 December 1889.

For many years "Admiral of the Swiss Navy" was considered a joke. Nevertheless during World War II an official version of the Swiss flag for use on water was adopted and today it is frequently seen, especially on the Rhine River and the lakes.

for the Battle of Laupen in 1339 "were marked with the sign of the Holy Cross, a white cross on a red shield...."

The flag began to take on its present form during the 19th century. The Napoleonic wars caused great upheavals in Switzerland and led to a revised political structure. When a new constitution was written for the confederation in 1848, the square red flag with a large white cross became standard for the army. The exact form of the present national flag dates from 12 December 1889.

2:3

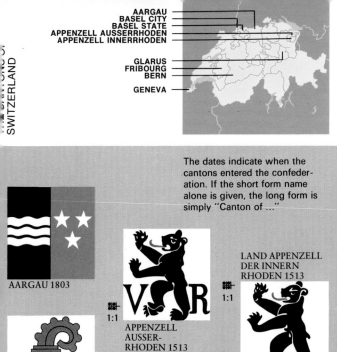

The dates indicate when the cantons entered the confederation. If the short form name alone is given, the long form is simply "Canton of ..."

AARGAU 1803

1:1

APPENZELL
AUSSER-
RHODEN 1513

BASEL-LANDSCHAFT
1501
BASEL STATE

1:1

BASEL-STADT 1501
BASEL CITY

FRIBOURG/
FREIBURG 1481

1:1

GENÈVE RÉPUBLIQUE
ET CANTON 1815
GENEVA
REPUBLIC
AND CANTON

LAND APPENZELL
DER INNERN
RHODEN 1513

1:1

BERN/BERNE 1553

1:1

GLARUS 1352

1:1

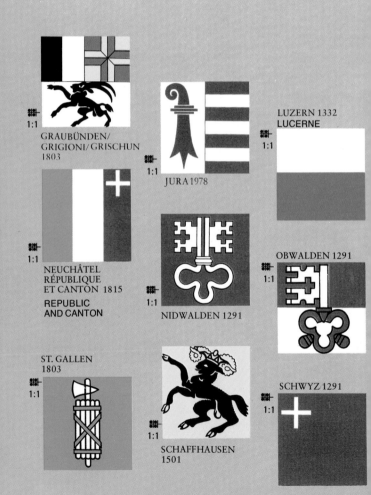

GRAUBÜNDEN/
GRIGIONI/ GRISCHUN
1803

JURA 1978

LUZERN 1332
LUCERNE

NEUCHÂTEL
RÉPUBLIQUE
ET CANTON 1815

REPUBLIC
AND CANTON

NIDWALDEN 1291

OBWALDEN 1291

ST. GALLEN
1803

SCHAFFHAUSEN
1501

SCHWYZ 1291

102

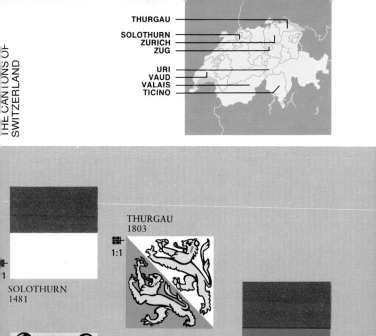

SOLOTHURN
1481

THURGAU
1803

1:1

TICINO 1803

1:1

URI 1291

VALAIS/WALLIS
1815

1:1

LIBERTE
ET
PATRIE

1:1

VAUD 1803

ZUG 1352

ZÜRICH 1351

1:1

STATE ARMS

The flag of Honduras recalls its former union with Guatemala, Nicaragua, El Salvador, and Costa Rica by the five stars added to the central stripe in 1866; the tradition of the stripes goes back even further into the past.

The blue-white-blue horizontally-striped flag of the United Provinces of

1:2
Officially adopted
18 January 1949.

1:2 ≈

Cornucopias for agricultural wealth; mountains, mines, and mining tools for its mineral wealth; and trees for its sylvan resources all figure in the arms adopted in 1866 and modified in 1935.

the Center of America, based on the Argentine flag, was first hoisted in the independence struggle against Spain on 4 July 1818, when the commodore of an Argentine squadron, Louis Aury, proclaimed the first independent Central American state on islands off the eastern coast of Nicaragua.

Aury's government lasted until 1821, when Central America proclaimed its independence. Although it first became part of the Mexican empire in 1823, when complete independence was established the new national flag had stripes similar to, and apparently based on, those of the first free state on Santa Catalina.

STATE ARMS

In 1293 when Prince Jayakatong led a revolt that ended the Kingdom of Singasari, a red and white flag was adopted by the new Majapahit Empire. Modern Indonesia looks back on that state as its predecessor and the source of its own *Merah-Putih* ("red-white") flag.

Its modern revival dates from 1922,

Officially hoisted
17 August
1945.

2:3 ≈

PRESIDENTIAL FLAG

1:1/4:5

for in that year the Indonesian Association formed by students in the Netherlands adopted the red-white flag. Taken up by the Indonesian Nationalist Party, it flew in Java for the first time in 1928. Indonesian independence, finally proclaimed at the end of World War II, required five more years of struggle before the new nation was recognized by the Dutch. Indonesia's date of independence is reflected in the seventeen wing feathers and eight tail feathers of the Garuda in its coat of arms. The star, padi, and the cotton of the arms are repeated as symbols in the presidential standard.

Symbols in the coat of arms stand for belief in God, popular sovereignty, national conscious-ness, social justice, and equality between men and women. The motto means "Unity in Diversity."

105

STATE ARMS

An archeological expedition found a small metallic flag in the ruins of the ancient city of Khabis in eastern Iran. It has been dated to 3000 B.C. and may be the oldest existing flag in the world. Among the emblems engraved on the Khabis flag are two lions and a sun. These have been common motifs throughout Iranian history: they have

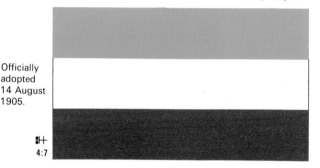

Officially adopted 14 August 1905.

4:7

Many nations have claimed the honor of having the oldest national flag—including Iran, Denmark, Mexico, Sri Lanka, Scotland, Latvia, the United States, Japan, Mali, Malta, and Austria. One problem in analyzing the question is that the concept of "national flag" as it is understood today does not go back beyond the late 18th century, even if some designs now used as national flags are considerably older. Also, many flags have changed in one detail or another and it is difficult to measure the degree of their continuity in deciding which can be considered the oldest.

been used in combination since at least the 13th century A.D. and a cloth flag showing the lion and sun is known from the 1400s.

At first associated with astrological and religious meanings, the lion and sun gradually came to be recognized as the national emblem of Iran. In the 19th century Iran's flag was white with the lion and sun inside borders of red and green. The basic tricolor pattern dates from the constitution of 14 August 1905, to which artistic alterations were made in 1912, 1933, and circa 1964.

The revolution which swept Iran in 1979 made no alteration in the national flag and arms up to the time of writing (April 1979).

STATE ARMS

In 1958 Iraq and Jordan were briefly linked in the Arab Union. The flag of that confederation was the second version of the Arab Revolt Flag (see the United Arab Emirates). It differed from the original only in having horizontal stripes of black-white-green instead of black-green-white; a red triangle was set at the hoist. That flag

Officially hoisted
31 July
1963.

2:3

was also used by Iraq with two white stars on the triangle—later changed to a trapezoid—in the 1920s.

In 1963 efforts were made by Iraq, Egypt, and Syria to reestablish the United Arab Republic. In anticipation of amalgamation, both Syria and Iraq altered their flags to the basic United Arab Republic design—red-white-black horizontal stripes with green stars in the center. The union failed to materialize, but the three stars of the Iraqi flag stand as a reminder of the aspiration to find common solutions to Arab problems.

The arms of Iraq, featuring the eagle of Saladin and the name of the state, are based on those used by the United Arab Republic from 1958 to 1971. Similar arms are used by the two Yemens, although none of the three was a member state of the UAR.

Saladin, the 12th century military and political leader, symbolizes Arab unity in the face of foreign threats to independence. The model for the eagle is a carving on the wall of a building in Cairo supposedly placed there on Saladin's order.

STATE ARMS

For centuries blue and white were considered the national colors of Iceland, appearing in national costume and elsewhere. In the first flag designs proposed for Iceland, these colors predominated; they were also found in the arms used between 1903 and 1919—a white falcon on a blue shield.

Officially hoisted 19 June 1915; restrictions on use at sea lifted 1 December 1918.

18:25

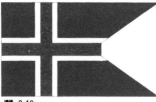

9:16

To indicate its links with other Scandinavian nations a Scandinavian cross flag was selected and the color red included when the definitive Icelandic flag design was established. At first the king of Denmark refused to approve the design; even when it became official, usage was restricted to land and to coastal waters.

The appearance of the flag was unchanged when Iceland became independent in 1919 and when it became a republic in 1944. Iceland has also followed the custom common in Scandinavia and the Baltic of employing a swallow-tailed flag shape for official purposes.

9:16 PRESIDENTIAL FLAG

MEDITERRANEAN SEA — SYRIA
Jerusalem ✴
EGYPT

STATE ARMS

On 21 July 1891 at the dedication of Zion Hall in Boston, Massachusetts, the B'nai Zion Educational Society displayed a flag based on the *tallis* or Jewish prayer shawl. It was white with blue stripes; in the center was the ancient *Magen David* (Shield of David, often erroneously called Star of David).

▶ P. 251

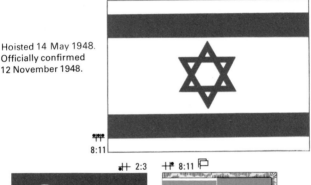

Hoisted 14 May 1948.
Officially confirmed
12 November 1948.

8:11

⚓ 2:3   ⚓ 8:11 ▭

⚓ 2:3   1:1 PRESIDENTIAL FLAG

STATE ARMS

Since Italy was among the first nations to take up the revolutionary principles espoused by France in 1789, it is not surprising that the French Tricolor was chosen as the model for Italy's own national flag. The substitution of green for blue in the stripe at the hoist is said to have been a decision made by Napoleon

Officially
adopted
19 June 1946.

2:3

PRESIDENTIAL
FLAG

1:1

himself.
Probably the first use of the colors is to be found in the uniforms of the Urban Militia of Milan. Following Napoleon's invasion of Lombardy in 1796, it became the National Guard and received a standard whose field consisted of vertical green, white, and red stripes.

▶ P. 2

2:3

2:3

CUBA

HAITI

Kingston ✶

CARIBBEAN SEA

STATE ARMS

Green is a symbol of hope and of agriculture, gold of natural wealth and the beauty of sunlight. Black stands for the past and present hardships facing the country.

The arms are those originally granted in 1661; the pattern was modified in 1957 by having the motto and artistic rendition altered.

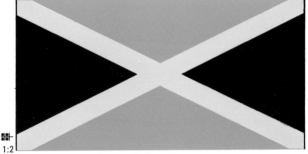

1:2

Officially hoisted 6 August 1962.

4:9

ROYAL FLAG

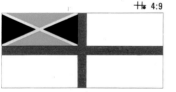

4:7 ≈

GOVERNOR-GENERAL'S FLAG

PRIME MINISTER'S FLAG

1:2 ≈

1:2 ≈

YUGOSLAVIA

STATE ARMS

The white, blue, and red have had two derivations: Imperial Russia, to which Slavs looked for support in seeking freedom from Austrian and Ottoman domination, flew a horizontal tricolor of white-blue-red. Also these same colors had appeared in the French republican banner familiar to Yugoslavs because its Illyrian area

1:2

In use since September 1941.
Officially adopted 31 January 1946.

PRESIDENTIAL FLAG

1:1

The date 29 November 1943 in the coat of arms recalls legislation adopted then which initiated the country's new social and political system. The torches are for the six constituent republics of Yugoslavia.

was annexed to France.

When the Kingdom of the Serbs, Croats, and Slovenes was proclaimed in 1918, the flag it adopted was blue-white-red with a coat of arms. Renamed Yugoslavia, the nation kept its flag unchanged. In September 1941, however, the partisans led by Josip Broz (Tito) replaced the royal arms with their own red star. Having liberated their land from fascism, the victorious partisans then officially confirmed the new flag on 31 January 1946. The partisan star has also been introduced as a symbol into other Yugoslav flags.

⊹ 2:3   ⊹ 2:3

Yugoslavia is one of many countries where the basic design of the national flag has been modified by governments of different ideologies through use of a special symbol.

In the past monarchist symbols appeared on the tricolors of Yugoslavia and its constituent parts in place of the red star of Communism. When Yugoslavia was dismembered in World War II, the fascist Ustashi inserted their party badge and the state arms in the flag of the Independent State of Croatia.

BOSNA I HERCEGOVINA
BOSNIA AND HERZEGOVINA

Officially adopted
31 December 1946.
The red is for
Communism.

1:2

CRNA GORA
MONTENEGRO

Officially adopted
31 December 1946.
The Montenegrin tricolor
dates from ca. 1880.

1:2

113

HRVATSKA
CROATIA

Officially adopted
18 January 1947.
The Croat tricolor dates
from 1848.

1:2

MAKEDONIJA
MACEDONIA

Officially adopted
31 December 1946.
The historical arms were
red with the gold lion.

1:2

SLOVENIJA
SLOVENIA

Officially adopted
16 January 1947.
The Slovene tricolor dates
from 1848.

1:2

Officially adopted
17 January 1947.
The Serbian tricolor dates
from 1835. The Auto-
nomous Province of
Vojvodina and the Auto-
nomous District of Kosovo
and Mitohija have no flags
of their own but use the
flag of Serbia, of which
they are a part.

SRBIJA
SERBIA

1:2

114

STATE ARMS

Communist forces seized control of Cambodia in 1975, and the following year the name of the country was changed to Democratic Kampuchea. Its flag is in harmony both with Communist traditions and Khmer precedents. The red field, symbolizing socialism and revolution, bears a representation of Angkor Wat, ''the

Officially adopted
5 January 1976.

2:3

2:3

The arms of Democratic Kampuchea comprise the name of the state written in Khmer on a red ribbon which enfolds sheaves of rice. Fields of rice, an irrigation system, and a factory stand for agriculture and industry.

Great Temple.'' One of the most impressive architectural structures in the world, it was built in the 14th century by the Khmer Empire, predecessors to modern Kampuchea.

Dissident forces backed by the Vietnamese army invaded the country and in January 1979 proclaimed the People's Republic of Kampuchea. The flag of the Kampuchean National United Front for National Salvation became the new national flag. Based on the flag flown 30 years previously by the Khmer Issarak rebels, it differs from the flag of Democratic Kampuchea in the number of towers in Angkor Wat. Civil war between the two governments continues at the time of writing (April 1979).

115

STATE ARMS

The long struggle for independence was led by the Kenya African National Union (KANU). In its flag horizontal stripes of black, red, and green symbolized the ethnic majority of Kenya, the blood they share in common with people everywhere, and the fertile fields and forests of the land.

In the national flag the same colors

Officially hoisted 12 December 1963.

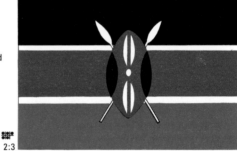

2:3

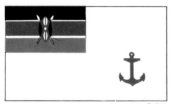

PRESIDENTIAL FLAG

5:9 ≈

stand for the people of Kenya, their struggle for independence, and agriculture and natural resources. White fimbriations for peace and unity were added to separate the three stripes of the KANU flag. The traditional Masai tribal shield and the spears symbolize defense of freedom.

The Swahili motto in the Kenyan coat of arms means "Let's Pull Together." Mount Kenya serves as a compartment for the arms, while lions symbolic of protection constitute the supporters. Examples of local agricultural produce frame the shield at the bottom.

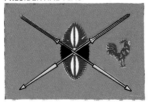

2:3

STATE ARMS

The coat of arms which had been granted on 1 May 1937 to the Gilbert and Ellice Islands Colony was un-altered, as used by the Gilbert Islands, following reconstitution of the Ellice Islands as the independent nation of Tuvalu. The motto (in both former national languages) means "Fear of God, Honor the King."

1:2

Officially hoisted July 1979.

Kiribati is the sole Commonwealth country to use an armorial banner, that is, a flag whose design corresponds exactly to the shield of its arms. In other parts of the world a number of countries represent their entire coat of arms some-where on the national flag or include the national flag as an element in the arms. Only Switzerland and Austria, how-ever, have true armorial banners—flags whose designs have been taken directly and without change from preexisting coats of arms.

Government-owned vessels of the Gilberts flew the British Blue Ensign defaced in the fly with a flag badge—in this case the shield of the arms—prior to independence. The custom arose in various British colonies of using this as the civil flag, represent-ing the colony in international sport events, regional meetings, etc. That practice was given legal sanction in the Gilbert and Ellice Islands as of 28 August 1969.

The frigate bird is part of the local fauna in the islands, while the Pacific is suggested by the heraldic represent-ation of water below a rising sun. The latter may indicate the geographical position of the islands, which straddle the International Date Line where a new day beings.

117

KOREA

STATE ARMS

The Korean Democratic People's Republic sees the white in its flag as a symbol of purity, strength, and dignity. White has, however, been the traditional color of the Korean nation for centuries. The blue stripes represent a commitment to peace, while the red indicates that the nation is on the path to socialism.

1:2

Officially adopted
8 September 1948.

Vladimir Lenin—Communist theoretician and leader of the Russian Revolution, which led to the establishment of the first Communist state in the world—was well aware that the success of his undertaking would not be complete until it affected the everyday lives and beliefs of individual citizens. His statement that "Communism is Soviet power plus electrification of the whole country" is reflected in the design of the arms of the Korean Democratic People's Republic.

The star is a symbol of the leading role played by the Korean Workers' Party in creating the new economic, social, and political structure of the country following World War II. Because Korea is basically an agricultural nation, sheaves of rice surround the coat of arms adopted by the Korean Democratic People's Republic in 1948. The sheaves are bound by a red ribbon bearing the name of the state. At the center is a landscape reflecting the country's determination to industrialize. A hydroelectric station and dam, perhaps the one built on the Amnokan River, figure prominently.

STATE ARMS

When the Exclusion Doctrine, which closed the country to foreign intercourse, was ended in 1876, Korea recognized the necessity of a national flag. The flag hoisted in August 1882, when the first envoys were sent to Japan, became official on 27 January 1883. It differed from the present flag only in minor details.

Officially adopted
25 January
1950.

2:3

PRESIDENTIAL FLAG   2:3

2:3 ≈

From 1910 to 1945 Korea was under Japanese occupation, followed by three years of American and Soviet administration. In 1948 the Republic of Korea reestablished the *t'aeguk* flag which was given its present form two years later.

Its white field stands for peace and the white clothing Koreans have traditionally worn.

The *t'aeguk* in the center resembles the yin and yang of Chinese philosophy and expresses the diversity of forces in the universe and their interaction. The *kwae* on either side correspond to the four cardinal directions, the seasons, and the sun, moon, earth, and heaven.

119

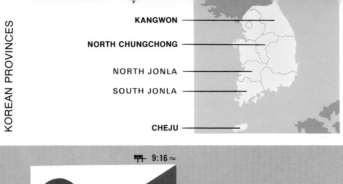

KOREAN PROVINCES

KANGWON

NORTH CHUNGCHONG

NORTH JONLA

SOUTH JONLA

CHEJU

해주 9:16 ≈

CHE-DJU
CHEJU
Officially hoisted 3 May 1966.

CHUNG-CHONG-PUK
NORTH CHUNGCHONG
Officially hoisted 1 February 1966.

충청북도

도 2:3

도 3:4

전 라 북 도

DJON-LA-NAM
SOUTH JONLA
Officially hoisted 31 July 1969.

DJON-LA-PUK
NORTH JONLA
Officially hoisted 1 July 1964.

도 2:3

도 2:3 ≈

KANG-WON
Officially hoisted 20 October 1962.

120

CYPRUS

STATE ARMS

Composed partially of Greek and partially of Turkish populations, Cyprus chose a flag of neutral design and colors when it became independent. The yellow color of the island is said to stand for the copper, mined since Roman days, which gave Cyprus its name. The olive branches below are for peace and prosperity; essentially

Officially hoisted 16 August 1960.

3:5

the same symbolism is reflected in the coat of arms.

The Cypriot national flag is rarely seen in the north of the island where the Turkish Federated State of Cyprus exists under the protection of troops from Turkey.

2:3

TURKISH FEDERATED STATE OF CYPRUS FLAG
(above) AND ARMS (right)

Certain parts of Cyprus known as the Sovereign Base Areas remain under the control of the former colonial power, Great Britain, and fly only the Union Jack.

STATE ARMS

When Kuwaiti independence was achieved in 1961 at the termination of the British protectorate, the pan-Arab colors were chosen for the new flag. Black is interpreted to mean the defeat of enemies on the battlefield, their blood leaving the swords of the Arabs red. Arab deeds are seen as white or pure, their lands green and

1:2

Officially hoisted 24 November 1961.

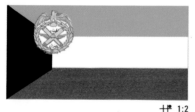

++ 1:2

ROYAL FLAG   1:2

fertile. That color symbolism derives from a poem written by Safi al-Din al-Hilli (1278–1349). He was born and died in what is modern Iraq and was a court poet in Egypt. The four colors have also been associated with historical Arab dynasties (see the United Arab Emirates).

A nation of seafarers and ship builders, Kuwait chose as the central emblem of its arms the traditional *dhow*. Falconry is a popular sport in the Persian Gulf, and the falcon in the arms is seen as a symbol of Kuwaiti prowess. The full name of the state is written at the top of the emblem.

BURMA
Luang
Prabang
* Vientiane
THAILAND
INDIAN OCEAN
SOUTH
CHINA
SEA
KAMPUCHEA

STATE ARMS

The distinctive three-headed white elephant which had long served as a symbol for Laos, a country known in the 14th century as Muong Lan Xang ("Land of a Million Elephants"), has disappeared. The red of that flag, which stood for the blood shed by the Lao people to obtain independence, is still present in the new flag.

Officially adopted
2 December 1975.

2:3

The dawn of a new day and industrialization are suggested by the sun and cogwheel at the bottom of the arms, immediately above the ribbon bearing the name of the country in Lao script. The words on either side proclaim "Peace, Independence, Democracy" and (to the right) "Unity, Prosperity, Social Progress." The socialist program of Laos is reflected in the hammer, sickle, and star at the top. Adopted in 1975, the arms are clearly based on long established patterns of Communist heraldry.

Originally used by the Lao Patriotic Front, that flag dates from the 1950s. Its broad blue stripe is an emblem of prosperity, the white disk signaling the promise of bright new future for the country. The disk is a common flag symbol in the Far East, appearing either as a sun or a wheel or the *yin-yang*, symbol of opposites. Such disks cut across ideological and religious lines to appear in the flags of Japan, both Koreas, Mongolia, the Republic of China, India, and several national flags no longer in existence. The colors of the Lao flag are also found in the flags of neighboring Burma, Thailand, China (until 1949), Cambodia (until 1976), and Malaysia.

123

STATE ARMS

The national dress of Lesotho includes a conical hat woven of straw. There are many varieties, but the hat silhouetted on the national flag is typical. The blue field stands for the sky and rain and the white symbolizes peace. Green and red are, respectively, for the land and faith.

These themes are reflected in the

Officially hoisted 4 October 1966.

2:3 ≈

ROYAL FLAG   2:3 ≈

The original draft of the Lesotho shield showed a representation of Moshoeshoe I. This was altered to a depiction of his personal and dynastic symbol, the crocodile, in the arms established at the time of Sotho independence.

motto of the national arms—"Peace, Rain, Plenty." Behind the traditional Sotho shield are 19th century weapons, the assegai and kerrie. When other black peoples of South Africa were being conquered by the British or Boers, King Moshoeshoe (pronounced moo *shway* shway) requested of Queen Victoria that he and his country "might rest under the great folds of her flag." Almost a century later Sotho independence was reestablished under King Moshoeshoe II. Thaba Bosiu (Mountain of Night), where Moshoeshoe I rallied his people and where in 1870 he was buried, is represented in the national coat of arms.

STATE ARMS

An American colony founded to provide a homeland for freed slaves returning to Africa from the United States, Liberia had had a flag since 1827. Understandably, the American flag constituted the basic design, except that a white cross substituted for the stars. In 1845 a Liberian ship flying that flag was seized by British

10:19

Officially adopted 26 July 1847.

PRESIDENTIAL FLAG

1:1

The dawn of a new day, the dove of peace, agricultural implements, and a ship such as that on which early colonists arrived are all represented in the Liberian national coat of arms.

authorities for lack of a recognized ensign; to give this flag international standing the decision was made to proclaim Liberian independence.

The basic form of the old flag was retained, but the number of stripes was reduced to eleven (the number of men signing the Liberian Declaration of Independence). A single white star on dark blue spoke of what was then the only independent nation in black Africa. The Liberian flag was designed and made by a committee consisting of seven women.

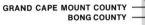

GRAND CAPE MOUNT COUNTY
BONG COUNTY

GRAND BASSA COUNTY
GRAND GEDEH COUNTY

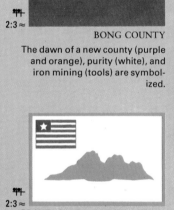

These flags were presented to the Liberian counties by President William V. S. Tubman on 29 November 1965, his seventieth birthday.

2:3 ≈

BONG COUNTY

The dawn of a new county (purple and orange), purity (white), and iron mining (tools) are symbolized.

2:3 ≈

GRAND CAPE MOUNT COUNTY

Grand Cape Mount appears against a white field of peace and purity.

2:3 ≈

GRAND BASSA COUNTY

Dark blue is for loyalty, the stripes for the four Grand Bassa men who signed Liberia's Declaration of Independence.

2:3 ≈

GRAND GEDEH COUNTY

The new county rises like its namesake mountain; white is for purity of heart, blue for peace and prosperity.

126

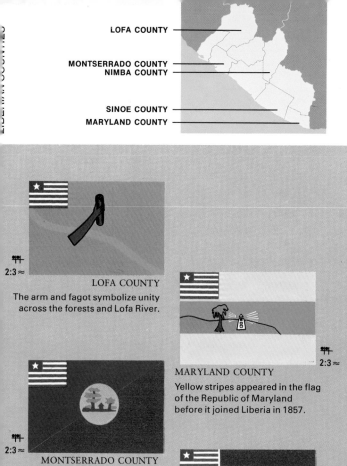

LOFA COUNTY

MONTSERRADO COUNTY
NIMBA COUNTY

SINOE COUNTY
MARYLAND COUNTY

2:3 ≈

LOFA COUNTY

The arm and fagot symbolize unity
across the forests and Lofa River.

2:3 ≈

MARYLAND COUNTY

Yellow stripes appeared in the flag
of the Republic of Maryland
before it joined Liberia in 1857.

2:3 ≈

MONTSERRADO COUNTY

Old and new cultures (blue and
red) met on the county's Provi-
dence Island.

NIMBA COUNTY

Valor, purity, and fidelity are
reflected in the flag's stripes.

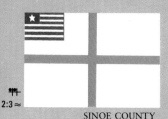

2:3 ≈

SINOE COUNTY

White and green correspond to
purity and tropical forests.

127

STATE ARMS

In 1971 Libya formed the Federation of Arab Republics with Egypt and Syria. The red-white-black horizontally striped flag with the gold arms of the Federation in the center was used in common by the three. (Libya had previously flown the same flag without any emblem.)

Although relations between Libya and

1:2≈

Officially adopted November 1977.

While history provides some examples of monochromatic national flags—e.g., Zanzibar (red, 1856–1963), France (white, 1815–1830), and Bolivia (green, 1854–1855)—they are uncommon, perhaps because of the limitations a single color places on possibilities for symbolism. Some monochromatic flags have traditional meanings—red being for danger or revolution; orange for Hinduism; yellow for quarantine and caution; white for peace or surrender; and black for mourning, protest, or anarchy.

Egypt deteriorated, no change was made in the flag from 1972 until 1977 when Egyptian President Anwar Sadat traveled to Israel. That visit was seen by the leader of the General Secretariat of Libya, Colonel Muammar al Qaddafi, as a betrayal of the fundamental commitment of all Arabs to an independent Palestinian state. The Libyan (i.e., Federation) flag was immediately replaced by a banner of plain green, probably to recall Colonel Qaddafi's promise of a Green Revolution transforming Libya into a self-sufficient food-producing country.

The national coat of arms follows the arms of the Federation of Arab Republics in its basic form.

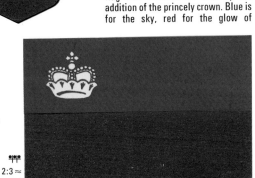

STATE ARMS

Blue and red were used as national colors in Liechtenstein during the 19th century and officially confirmed in the constitution of 1921. To avoid potential international confusion with the flag of Haiti, the Liechtenstein flag was modified in 1937 by the addition of the princely crown. Blue is for the sky, red for the glow of

Officially hoisted 25 July 1957.

2:3 ≈

evening fires, and the crown for the unity of the people, princely house, and nation.

PRINCELY FLAG   2:3 ≈

PRINCELY ARMS

The quarterings of the arms indicate the lineage of the ruling house by combining the shields of Silesia, the Kuenrings, Troppau, and East Frisia-Rietberg, with the horn of Jägerndorf at the bottom.

Lebanon has no official coat of arms.

In the eighteenth and nineteenth centuries Maronite Christians in Lebanon used a white flag bearing a cedar. This tree—symbolizing holiness, eternity, and peace—is native to the area and is mentioned several times in the Bible. Psalms 92:12 asserts that the "righteous shall grow... like a cedar in Lebanon." The

Officially adopted 7 December 1943.

2:3 ≈

red and white colors are those associated, respectively, with the Kayssites and Yemenites, opposing clans that divided Lebanese society between 634 and 1711.

During World War I the Lebanese Legion in French military service displayed a red saltire on a white flag, a cedar being represented in the center. Under the League of Nations mandate given to France, Lebanon displayed the French Tricolor with a cedar in the center; in 1943 when complete independence was gained the present flag was adopted.

Lebanon is one of a number of countries where official details of the flag are frequently ignored. The law provides that the cedar should touch the red stripes and be equal to one-third the length of the flag, but frequently it is shown considerably smaller. The traditional view has been that a flag is proper so long as it includes the essential design elements of colors and symbols, regardless of artistic rendition.

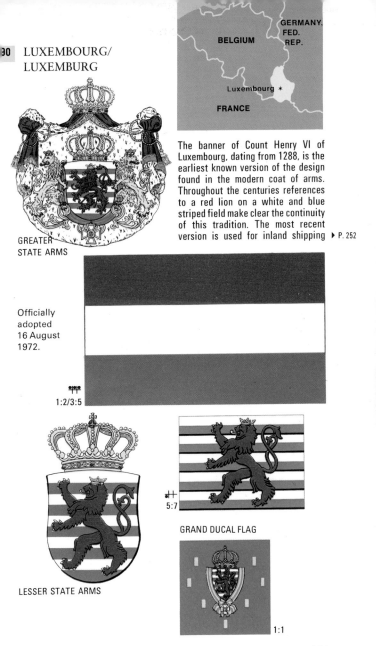

The banner of Count Henry VI of Luxembourg, dating from 1288, is the earliest known version of the design found in the modern coat of arms. Throughout the centuries references to a red lion on a white and blue striped field make clear the continuity of this tradition. The most recent version is used for inland shipping ▶ P. 252

GREATER
STATE ARMS

Officially
adopted
16 August
1972.

1:2/3:5

LESSER STATE ARMS

GRAND DUCAL FLAG

5:7

1:1

131

MOROCCO

ROYAL ARMS

A number of Arab dynasties throughout Moroccan history were characterized by specific colors appearing as the fields of their military flags on which Koranic inscriptions were written. From the 11th century until the beginning of the 17th, the principal color was white, under the Almoravids, Marinids, and Saadians.

Officially adopted 17 November 1915.

2:3

⊕ 2:3

Prior to 1915 the national flag of Morocco was plain red—a flag also used at that time by Oman, Zanzibar, and a number of small states in Indonesia, India, and Africa.

The red flags of the current dynasty have been used for the past 300 years. Sometimes an emblem was added, but it was only in 1915 that the green Seal of Solomon was officially established. By then France and Spain had divided Morocco into five parts, and it was not until 1969 that the last of many colonial flags was lowered, leaving a single national flag in all parts of Morocco.

The Atlas Mountains of northern Morocco appear in the center of the royal arms. The inscription at the bottom reads "If You Assist God, He Will Also Assist You."

STATE ARMS

Tradition relates that Árpád, a ninth-century Hungarian ruler whose dynasty lasted 400 years, displayed a plain red flag. Hungarians also believe that a double-barred cross was given by the Pope to St.Stephen, an early 11th century king, thus introducing the color white into the national coat of arms.

Officially hoisted
1 October
1957.

2:3 ≈

By the 15th century the Hungarian arms consisted of red and white horizontal stripes on the dexter half of a shield and the white cross, rising from green hills, on the red sinister. The green of the present national flag apparently derives from the color of the hills in the arms, as well as from military banners of the Hungarian army.

The influence of the French Revolution inspired use of the red, white, and green in three equal stripes. The Hungarian tricolor was in widespread use by the time of its first official adoption in 1848.

Hungarian national traditions are reflected in the red-white-green ribbon and shield of the coat of arms. Wheat, to symbolize the agricultural basis of the economy, was first introduced into the Hungarian arms following the establishment of the people's republic in 1949. The red star at the top, a symbol of Communism, first appeared in 1919 when a Soviet regime briefly ruled Hungary.

133

STATE ARMS

As in many other African and Asian countries, the national flag in Malawi is based directly on the flag of the political movement which led the country to independence. The flag adopted by the Malawi Congress Party in 1953 differs from that used by Malawi itself only in the absence of the rising sun emblem.

Officially
hoisted
6 July 1964.

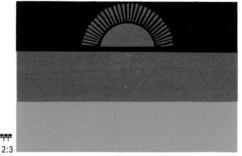

2:3

The sun has figured as an emblem in Malawi since 1914, when a coat of arms was granted by Royal Warrant to Nyasaland. (That name was replaced a half century later by Malawi—meaning "flaming waters," a reference to reflections of the sun in the surface of Lake Nyasa.) The theme of the sun was perhaps suggested by the Latin motto of Nyasaland, meaning "a light in the shadows." In any event it figured again in the arms granted to the short-lived Federation of Rhodesia and Nyasaland whose demise led to the independence of Malawi. In the current national arms the sun appears in both crest and shield.

In 1964, when its independence was obtained, Malawi added the sun to symbolize the dawning of a new day for Africa. The black stripe on which it rests stands for the people of the continent, and the red is for the blood of African martyrs in the cause of freedom. Green refers specifically to Malawi and the richness of its fields and forests.

The coat of arms of Malawi was granted by Queen Elizabeth II on 30 June 1964. Mount Mlanje, the tallest in the nation, appears as the compartment, while Lake Nyasa is symbolized by the wavy lines in the shield and crest. The fish eagle, leopard, and lions recall the abundant wildlife of Malawi.

STATE ARMS

Yellow is considered a royal color in Malaysia; red and white figure in the flags of other Southeast Asian states. Blue was chosen for the Malaysian flag to show its association with the Commonwealth, while the star and crescent indicate that the majority of the population is of the Muslim faith. United in 1948, Malaya hoisted its

1:2
Officially hoisted
16 September 1963.

first national flag on 26 May 1950. No change was introduced in 1957 when it became independent, but the addition of new states in 1963 altered the national name and flag. Two years later Singapore was excluded from the Federation but no alteration was made in the flag. The motto in the national arms, in Roman and Javi scripts, means ''Unity is Strength.''

1:2

ROYAL FLAG   ⊹⊦ 1:2

⊦⊹ 1:2

135

KEDAH

KELANTAN

PAHANG

NEGRI SEMBILAN
MALACCA
JOHORE

JOHOR

JOHORE   ⊬ 1:2

KEDAH

⊬ 1:2

KELANTAN

⊬ 1:2

MELAKA

⊬ 1:2   MALACCA

NEGERI SEMBILAN

NEGERI SEMBILAN   ⊬ 1:2

PAHANG

⊬ 1:2

Some of the state flags derive from monochromatic banners used in the past, while those of Malacca and Sarawak are based on the national flag. The coats of arms of Penang and Sabah inspired the flags of those states.

136

PERAK

⚓ 1:2

PULAU PINANG

PENANG ⚓ 1:2

SARAWAK

⚓ 3:5

TRENGGANU

⚓ 1:2

PERLIS

⚓ 1:2

SABAH

⚓ 1:2

SELANGOR

⚓ 1:2

137

STATE ARMS

The inspiration for the design of the Mali national flag is clear. Being under French colonial rule, citizens of the future nation were familiar with the Tricolor of France and patterned their own national flag after it. It is quite similar to the flags of other French colonies which became independent at roughly the same

Officially
adopted
1 March 1961.

2:3

time—Senegal, Guinea, Cameroon, Togo, and the Congo.

The colors in the flags of all these African countries are the same—green, yellow, and red. The pan-African colors, as they are known, were probably influenced by the flags of two African countries which had previously gained independence, Ethiopia and Ghana. Probably even more important as an influence was the fact that green, yellow, and red were the party colors of the African Democratic Rally, which led Mali to independence.

Mali has never adopted a coat of arms. Its seal bears the national motto—"One People, One Goal, One Faith."

Upon gaining independence in 1960, the French Sudan chose the name Mali, which had been used hundreds of yers before by a powerful empire.

Another ancient symbol—a stylized figure of a man known as the *kanaga*—was also adopted. Shown in black in the center of the first Mali flag, it recalled the continuous use of that symbol in Mali for 2,000 years. Muslim purists who objected to the representation of a human form successfully campaigned for its omission from the flag.

ITALY

SICILY

TUNISIA

★ Valletta

MEDITERRANEAN SEA

REPUBBLIKA TA' MALTA

STATE ARMS

A simple vertical bicolor, Malta's original flag, is reputed to date back to Count Roger the Norman, who took Malta from the Muslims in 1090. Adaptations have been used through the centuries: for example, it provided the basis for the arms and flag badge which were official in the latter part of British rule, which extended from

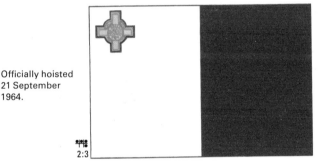

Officially hoisted 21 September 1964.

2:3

2:3

Mediterranean sun, a winnowing fork and shovel, the prickly-pear shrub, and a Maltese boat with the "eye of Osiris" painted on its prow were considered to have a more direct and more easily perceived relationship to the actual life of the people than the traditional arms formerly in use.

1814 to 1964. The distinctive Maltese cross characteristic of the Knights of St. John of Jerusalem, who ruled from 1530 to 1798, figures in the civil ensign of Malta.

As an augmentation of honor for its valiant resistance to enemy attack in World War II, Malta received royal permission on 28 December 1943 to add the George Cross to its arms and flag. Originally set against a blue canton, the cross now is separated from the white stripe only by a red fimbriation, as required by the laws of heraldry. The cross disappeared entirely from the coat of arms when a new design was adopted in 11 July 1975 following proclamation of a republic.

STATE ARMS

The blue of the national flag refers to the waters of the Indian Ocean which surround the island. The green land of Mauritius, the red of blood shed in the independence struggle, and the golden light of that independence are expressed in the other stripes of the flag.

Granted in 1906, the arms refer to

Officially hoisted 12 March 1968.

2:3

1:2

colonization from abroad (a ship), tropical vegetation (palm tree), and the strategic position of the island (the emblems referred to in the Latin motto, which translates as "The Star and Key of the Indian Ocean"). The supporters are the sambur deer, imported from Java in 1639, and the indigenous dodo bird which became extinct later in the 17th century.

1:2

1:2

GOVERNOR-GENERAL'S FLAG

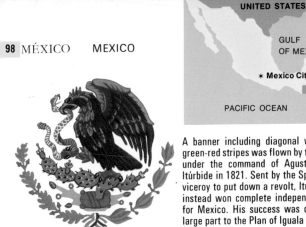

UNITED STATES

GULF
OF MEXICO

★ **Mexico City**

PACIFIC OCEAN

STATE ARMS

A banner including diagonal white-green-red stripes was flown by troops under the command of Agustín de Itúrbide in 1821. Sent by the Spanish viceroy to put down a revolt, Itúrbide instead won complete independence for Mexico. His success was due in large part to the Plan of Iguala which encompassed three guarantees—

Officially
hoisted
16 September
1968.

4:7

According to legend, the Mexica tribesmen were ordered by their sun god to settle where they should see a cactus growing from a rock. When they found this omen about 1325, they founded the settlement which later became Mexico City. By the time the Spaniards conquered Mexico in 1521 the iconographic emblem of that legend—the form of the rock, cactus, eagle, and snake—had become widely used. Suppressed under Spanish rule, it was revived with the independence movement of the early 19th century and has figured in almost every Mexican flag since that time.

religion, independence, union. This slogan meant that the conservatives accepted independence provided that the established religion (which guaranteed their social, political, and economic dominance) continue and that there would be a union of all Mexicans (Spanish, Indian, and those of mixed blood) rather than a policy of majority rule.

The Flag of the Three Guarantees, adopted on 2 November 1821, is probably based on the French Tricolor. It showed stripes of green (for independence), white (for the purity of religion), and red (the Spanish national color, for union) with the arms in the center.

MEDITERRANEAN SEA

Cairo ★

SAUDI ARABIA

LIBYA

RED SEA

SUDAN

STATE ARMS

The red, white, and black recall Egypt's revolution, its bright future, and the dark days of the past. The basic design originated in Egypt's Arab Liberation Flag, hoisted after King Faruq was deposed in 1952; in the center that flag showed the gold eagle of Saladin (see Iraq). In 1958 the United Arab Republic, formed by

Officially hoisted 1 January 1972.

2:3

the union of Egypt and Syria, had the same flag with two green stars replacing the eagle. No change was made when Syria ended the union in 1961, but a decade later the hawk of Quraish was substituted in the center. The Arab Liberation Flag had served as a model for other Arab national flags.

2:3

2:3

PRESIDENTIAL FLAG

2:3 ≈

MOZAMBIQUE

STATE ARMS

The Front for the Liberation of Mozambique had a flag which, unofficially, served as the national flag between 5 September 1974 and 25 June 1975. It had horizontal stripes of green, black, and yellow separated by white and a red triangle at the hoist. Those colors, repeated in the current flag, stand for agricultural wealth,

Officially hoisted 25 June 1975.

5:8 ≈

+⊞ 5:8 ≈ ▢

PRESIDENTIAL FLAG

2:3

the African continent, mineral wealth, justice and peace, and the revolutionary armed struggle against colonialism.

The rifle in the flag and arms is for defense and vigilance; the hoe for the peasantry and their agricultural output; the book for education; the cogwheel for the working class and industry; and the red star to symbolize the internationalist spirit of the Mozambique revolution. In addition the arms add a map of the country, its name on a ribbon, a rising sun for the new life which the revolution has brought, and sheaves of corn and sugar cane.

143

ITALY

FRANCE

★ Monaco

MEDITERRANEAN SEA

PRINCELY ARMS

There is a tradition that the original Grimaldis, whose heirs rule Monaco to this day, were able to capture the fortress dressed as monks, their swords hidden under their cassocks. This explains the supporters in the arms and the motto "With God's Aid."

The flag colors of Monaco are attest-

Officially adopted
4 April 1881.

4:5

ed as far back as 1339, although not in their present form. Banners of red and white lozenges—a design based on the arms—are found in the seventeenth century. On land it has been common since the last century to paint the pole from which the Monegasque flag is displayed with a red and white spiral.

The arms of Monaco took their present form in the 1800s, although the basic form dates back hundreds of years. The shield is surrounded by a representation of the Order of St. Charles. The cipher of Prince Rainier figures on his personal flag.

4:5

5:6 ≈

PRINCELY FLAG

STATE ARMS

The revolutionary path and socialist program of the Mongolian People's Republic, dating from 1924, is expressed graphically in the red stripes and gold star of the flag. Red banners had been carried by troops in 1921 under the leadership of Sukhe Bator and Choibalsan, the founders of modern Mongolia. Light blue has for

1:2

Officially confirmed 23 February 1949.

Mystical interpretations have been given to the *soyonbo* throughout Mongolian history. Today the flame at the top is seen as a promise of prosperity and progress. The sun and moon (as in the flag of Nepal) promise everlasting life for the nation. The triangles are arrowheads, threatening death to enemies of the people. The horizontal bars are for honesty and righteousness, the vertical ones for independence and strength. The ancient yin-yang symbol of the universe is here interpreted as two fish, an emblem of watchfulness on behalf of the state by men and women.

centuries been considered the Mongolian national color.

Along the hoist of the flag and at the top of the state arms appears the ancient symbol of Mongolia, called the *soyonbo*. Also in the arms are the wheat and cogwheel of agriculture and industry, linked by a ribbon bearing the initials of the state name. The landscape includes in stylized form the desert, steppe, and forest regions of Mongolia. The horseman racing into the sun—whose golden rays betoken prosperity—stands for the nation's advance toward Communism.

ROYAL ARMS

Red and white figured in the first national flags of Thailand; blue is associated with the king's birthday. The choice of colors is said to have been made to correspond to the same red, white, and blue found in the flags of Thailand's World War I allies— Britain, France, the United States, and Russia. The white of this *Trairong*

Officially adopted 28 September 1917.

2:3

("Tricolor") symbolizes the purity of the people protected by their religion. The blood sacrificed by Thais for their nation is reflected in the red stripes. The mythical Garuda in the royal standard is the enemy of all poisonous things and bearer of the god of bravery. The yellow is for Buddhism.

2:3

2:3

ROYAL STANDARD

1:1

146

MAURITANIE

MAURITANIA

ATLANTIC
OCEAN

MOROCCO

ALGERIA

MALI

★ Nouakchott

STATE SEAL

The message of the flag and arms of Mauritania, emphasized by the official name of the state, is clear: both the color green and the star and crescent emblem symbolize Islam, the religion of the majority of the population. The green and gold colors of the flag also recall the pan-African red-yellow-green flags of nations to

Officially
adopted
1 April 1959.

2:3

The northwest part of Mauritania comprises the lower portion of the former colony of Spanish Sahara, formally divided between Mauritania and Morocco on 14 April 1976.
Local nationalist forces under the leadership of Polisario had proclaimed the Sahara Arab Democratic Republic on 27 February 1976. Its flag is composed of black-white-green horizontal stripes, a red triangle at the hoist, and a red star and crescent on the central stripe. Polisario continues to struggle for the independence of the Sahara under this flag.

the south and the fact that Mauritania itself has a considerable black population, in addition to its Moorish majority.
Although France had previously discouraged the creation of local symbols within its colonial empire, following the establishment in 1958 of the Fifth Republic that policy was reversed. Thus both the flag and arms of Mauritania were adopted in advance of its independence, achieved on 28 November 1960. In addition to the name of the state in both official languages, the seal bears a palm tree and two slips of millet. The reverse of the seal has a different design.

STATE ARMS

Since the independence of Burma from Britain in 1948, its traditional color (orange) and peacock emblem have been little used. The star of independence originated during the struggle with the Japanese who occupied the country in World War II: the flag of the Anti-Fascist Resistance Movement was red with a

Officially hoisted 3 January 1974.

5:9

white star in the upper hoist.

The first flag of independent Burma surrounded that white star with five smaller ones, all on a dark blue canton. This color symbolized peace and tranquility; the white purity, honesty, and truth. The red was seen as a symbol of courage, solidarity, and tenacity of purpose.

The transformation of the country in 1974 into a socialist republic led to modifications of the flag. The gearwheel and rice are emblems of industry and agriculture. Instead of five stars for the principal ethnic groups, the flag now has fourteen stars, one for each state in the union.

Framing the central emblem of the arms and protecting it are two mythological lions known as *chinthe*. Familiar forms in ancient Burmese architecture, these lions incarnate ancient wisdom, bravery and strength, and purity and balance in the use of power. The ribbon below the feet of the lions is inscribed with the official name of the state; a map of Burma appears in the center.

STATE ARMS

VIRIBUS UNITIS

Following World War II South Africa refused to transfer its League of Nations mandate, which gave it legal authority over South West Africa, to the trusteeship system of the United Nations. Consequently that international organization has called for the independence of South West Africa, which it calls Namibia, although South Africa continues to administer it as a dependency under its own flag.

The liberation movements of Namibia have distinctive flags of their own. At the time of writing (April 1979) negotiations between the United Nations and South Africa are being conducted which may lead to its independence with a national flag of its own. The South Africans have already created a coat of arms featuring the flora, fauna, mineral resources, and history of the territory. They have also organized Namibian ethnic groups into separate territories with symbols of their own, including flags.

CAPRIVI   2:3

KAVANGO   2:3

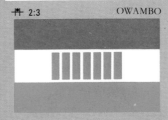

2:3   OWAMBO

STATE ARMS

PACIFIC OCEAN

PAPUA NEW GUINEA

SOLOMON ISLANDS

AUSTRALIA

The geographical position and people of Nauru find graphic expression in the symbolism of its flag. The island is just one degree south of the equator in the Pacific Ocean to the west of the International Date Line, hence the yellow horizontal stripe on blue and the off-center star immediately below the stripe. The twelve points of the

1:2

Officially hoisted 31 January 1968.

star are for the 12 tribes of Nauru—the Eamwit, Eamwidamit, Emea, Eano, Emangum, Eoaru, Eamwidara, Deiboe, Ranibok, Iruwa, Irutsi, and Iwi. The latter two tribes are now extinct.

Many flags proposed prior to independence reflected the design of the Australian national flag, which flew over the island during several decades of trusteeship administration. The dark blue field and white multipointed star chosen indicate such influence. It was designed by a Nauruan in a competition held locally to create a flag, the final graphic rendition being done by an Australian flag manufacturer, Evan Evans Pty. Ltd.

The economic base of the nation is the deposit of guano which is being mined for phosphates. The chemical symbol for phosphorus appropriately appears in the chief of the arms, above a frigate bird and a spray of tomano flowers. Cocoa palm fronds frame the shield, while above is part of the ceremonial insignia of the Nauru chief, constructed of plaited fiber cords, local seeds, sharks' teeth, and frigate bird feathers. The frigate bird is frequently kept as a pet by Nauruans.

NETHERLANDS

STATE AND ROYAL ARMS

The flag of the Water Beggars—who figured prominently in the Dutch war of independence that began in the late 16th century—had horizontal stripes of orange-white-blue. It was called the Prince's Flag in honor of William I, Prince of Orange, and the colors were probably taken from his livery. The battle cry of the Dutch,

In use since the sixteenth century; confirmed by Royal Decree 19 February 1937.

2:3

ROYAL STANDARD

1:1

The royal flag shows the dynastic colors orange (Orange) and blue (Nassau); elements of the national arms; the Military Order of William; and a horn referring to the legendary William with a Horn of the eighth century.

referring both to the stripe in their flag and the princely house to which they had entrusted their fortunes, was "Orange on Top!"

By the time Spain recognized Dutch freedom in 1648, the top stripe of the flag of the United Provinces was beginning to change from orange to red, although in that era there were many variations of design. The first law officially adopting the red-white-blue was issued on 14 February 1796 by the Batavian Republic, as the country was then known. It was readopted by the Kingdom of Holland in 1806 and, following liberation from French occupation, was reestablished on 16 March 1816.

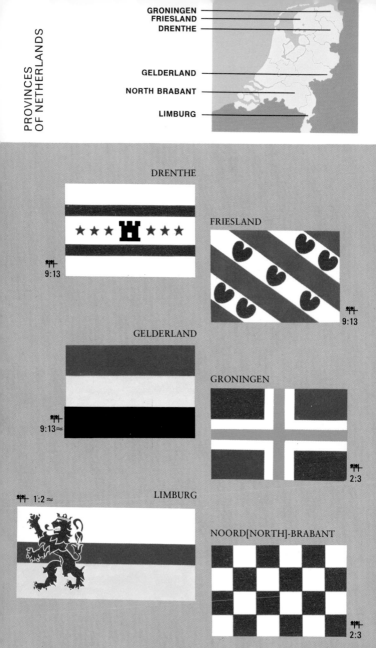

GRONINGEN
FRIESLAND
DRENTHE

GELDERLAND
NORTH BRABANT

LIMBURG

DRENTHE

9:13

FRIESLAND

9:13

GELDERLAND

9:13 ≈

GRONINGEN

2:3

LIMBURG

1:2 ≈

NOORD[NORTH]-BRABANT

2:3

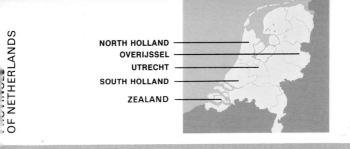

NORTH HOLLAND
OVERIJSSEL
UTRECHT
SOUTH HOLLAND
ZEALAND

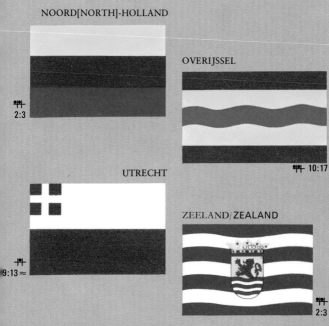

NOORD[NORTH]-HOLLAND

2:3

OVERIJSSEL

10:17

UTRECHT

9:13 ≈

ZEELAND/ZEALAND

2:3

ZUID[SOUTH]-HOLLAND

2:3

Lions appear in a number of Dutch provincial flags and arms. The lion in the national arms holds a sword and bundle of arrows to symbolize protection of the rights of Dutch provinces through their unity and constitutional government. This is also emphasized in the motto "I Will Maintain" in those arms.

153

STATE ARMS

PUERTO RICO

CARIBBEAN SEA

★ Willemstad

VENEZUELA

The motto in the coat of arms adopted on 6 November 1964 indicates that the islands are "United by Liberty." The crown suggests the political status of the Netherlands Antilles as a self-governing part of the Kingdom of the Netherlands. The stars represent the six islands—Aruba, Bonaire, Curaçao, St. Martin, Saba,

Officially hoisted 15 December 1959.

2:3

GOVERNOR'S FLAG   2:3

and St. Eustatius. Aruba and Curaçao have coats of arms of their own and the former has a flag, hoisted on 18 March 1976.

The flag of the Netherlands Antilles was hoisted on the fifth anniversary of its achievement of autonomy. It is flown subordinate to the Dutch flag and may not be decorated with the orange pennant which surmounts the Netherlands national flag on certain holidays. Close links with the metropolitan power are also reflected in the color shades defined in both the Dutch and Antillian flag as "bright vermilion" and "cobalt blue." Scientific designations of the shades are based on specifications prepared by the Central Standardization Bureau at The Hague.

ARUBA   2:3

STATE ARMS

ROYAL ARMS

ROYAL FLAG

The crossed swords are the *khukari* used by the Gurkha soldier in combat. Other charges are the sacred cow, pheasant, rhododendron, and motto "Mother and Motherland Are Dearer Than Heaven."

Official specifications issued in 1962 eliminated the facial features from the sun and moon and gave highly detailed measurements for all the dimensions of the flag, but it did not entirely "modernize" this banner. Nepal remains the only country in the world without a rectangular national flag. The two tails are said to rep-

4:3 ≈

Officially adopted
16 December 1962.

resent the peaks of the Himalayas. Crimson is the Nepali national color and dark blue and red frequently appear in religious and profane art in this country. The sun and moon express the hope that the nation may live as long as those celestrial bodies. Both the state and royal arms include diverse religious symbols—the footprints of the Buddha (born in what is now Nepal), the trident of Vishnu, the temple of Lord Pasupadineth, destroyer of evil. The background landscape represents the country from the lowlands in the south to the Himalayas in the north.

2:3 ≈

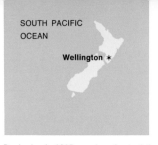

SOUTH PACIFIC
OCEAN

Wellington ⚹

STATE ARMS

Beginning in 1865 a series of colonial ensigns—red for merchant ships and blue for government vessels—spread with the growth of the British Empire. Local symbols added at the fly end of these flags often were much older: the stars of New Zealand, for example, date back at least to 1834, when they figured in the national flag

1:2
Officially adopted 12 June 1902.

⊹ 1:2

⊹ 1:2

of the United Tribes of New Zealand, a Maori state that proclaimed its independence on 28 October 1835. This was white with a red cross, the canton bearing four white eight-pointed stars between the arms of a black-bordered red cross, all on a blue background. When Britain assumed sovereignty over New Zealand in 1840 the Union Jack was hoisted.

The 1865 Colonial Naval Defense Act prompted consideration of a special badge to display on the Blue Ensign. Although the four stars of the Southern Cross were suggested, the design actually approved on 10 January 1867 simply had the letters NZ. The design of the present flag dates from 23 October 1869, al-

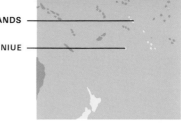

COOK ISLANDS

NIUE

17:19 ≈

ROYAL FLAG

GOVERNOR-GENERAL'S FLAG   1:2

COOK ISLANDS

⁂ 1:2

NIUE

⁂ 1:2

though at the time it was limited in usage to government owned vessels. Although a number of other nations—Brazil, Australia, and Western Samoa, for example—use the Southern Cross constellation on their flags and/or arms, the particular arrangement chosen for the New Zealand flag is unique.

A New Zealand Red Ensign for use on merchant ships went into effect on 1 January 1900: its red field had a white disk with four red stars. A similar disk was added to the Blue Ensign, replacing the former pattern of white-fimbriated red stars on a blue field. Interest in the subject and disagreement over the best design led to parliamentary action. A law promulgated in 1902 provided that the 1869 flag should be "the recognized flag of the colony for general use on shore within the colony and on all vessels belonging to the Government of New Zealand." The following year the civil ensign was modified to its present form. The New Zealand White Ensign for use on warships did not replace the British White Ensign until 1968.

The Cook Islands flag dates from 1973, although as an independent country and protectorate it formerly had several other flags. The flag of Niue is the first for that island and the first national flag of the British ensign type to have a yellow field. It was adopted in 1975.

157

STATE ARMS

The flag and arms of Nicaragua are almost exactly like those originally adopted in 1823 by the United Provinces of the Center of America. The independence of that state was proclaimed on 15 September 1821, but in January 1822 Emperor Iturbide of Mexico annexed the area, and freedom was not reestablished until

Officially hoisted 27 August 1971.

3:5

3:5

June of 1823. Nicaragua reestablished the blue-white-blue after briefly substituting a flag of yellow, white, and mother of pearl.

The five volcanoes correspond to the five nations of the isthmus, washed by the waters of the Caribbean Sea and Pacific Ocean. Rays of liberty spreading throughout the land are shed by the liberty cap. The rainbow is for peace, and the triangle on which the entire design is represented symbolizes equality. Two related forces influenced the choice of these symbols—the French Revolution and Masonry.

The flag is related to those of El Salvador, Guatemala, Honduras, and Costa Rica. Their common inspiration apparently was the flag of Argentina.

3 NIGER

STATE ARMS

Vast portions of the east and north of Niger are part of the Sahara Desert, a region symbolized by the orange stripe of the flag. The grassy plains of the south and west—the latter nourished by the river from which the country takes its name—are the basis for the green stripe. Green also stands for fraternity and hope.

Officially adopted
23 November 1959.

6:7 ≈

Orange being a very uncommon flag color, it is surprising that four of the flags incorporating orange should be quite similar in design. India displays a wheel instead of the sun, which appears in the flag of Niger, and the Ivory Coast and Ireland have vertical stripes with no emblem at all on the white. Yet all four flags are basically orange-white-green tricolors. The historical sources and symbolisms of these four flags are nevertheless quite distinct, and they were adopted quite independently of one another.

The sun in the center is described as a symbol of the willingness of the Nigerois people to sacrifice themselves in defending their rights. White is both the good conscience of those who have done their duty and the mark of purity and innocence.

The sun is repeated in the coat of arms, where it is surrounded with emblems of animal husbandry and farming—a buffalo head and millet blades. The military valor of the people in the great empires of the past, ancestors of the modern Nigerois, is suggested by the crossed Touareg swords and spear.

159

NIGER

CHAD

* Lagos

GULF OF GUINEA

STATE ARMS

Flying over his native land on his way to London for university work, M.T.S. Akinkunmi was impressed by the virgin green land below him. He chose that color as the primary symbol for Nigeria in the flag he designed which was the winner in a contest that drew almost 3,000 entries.

The white stripe in the center sig-

1:2

Officially hoisted 1 October 1960.

1:2

nifies peace; the green stands for agriculture, which remains the backbone of the national economy. The red sun that Akinkunmi had included on the white stripe was omitted by the committee that approved the design for independence.

In the Nigerian arms black is said to refer to the rich soil of the land— irrigated by the Niger and Benue rivers whose confluence is expressed heraldically by the Y-shaped ''pall wavy argent.'' An eagle for strength and horses for dignity serve as the crest and supporters.

LAGOS STATE

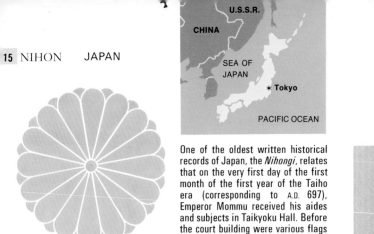

IMPERIAL ARMS

One of the oldest written historical records of Japan, the *Nihongi*, relates that on the very first day of the first month of the first year of the Taiho era (corresponding to A.D. 697), Emperor Mommu received his aides and subjects in Taikyoku Hall. Before the court building were various flags bearing (among other symbols) the ▶ P. 252

Officially adopted
5 August
1854.

2:3 ≈

+ 9:11 ≈   + 2:3

IMPERIAL FLAG   2:3   2:3 ≈   PRIME MINISTER'S FLAG

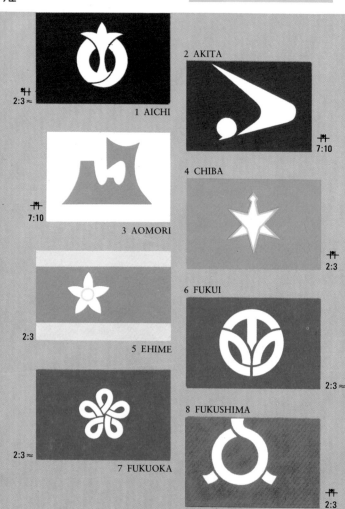

2:3 ≈

1 AICHI

2 AKITA

7:10

7:10

3 AOMORI

4 CHIBA

2:3

2:3

5 EHIME

6 FUKUI

2:3 ≈

2:3 ≈

7 FUKUOKA

8 FUKUSHIMA

2:3

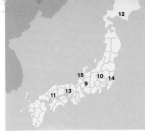

9 GIFU

10 GUMMA

11 HIROSHIMA

12 HOKKAIDO

13 HYOGO

14 IBARAKI

15 ISHIKAWA

3 ≈

7:10

2:3

2:3

2:3

1:44

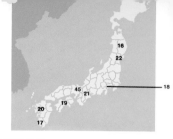

2:3 ≈

16 IWATE

17 KAGOSHIMA

2:3

7:10

18 KANAGAWA

19 KOCHI

2:3 ≈

20 KUMAMOTO

2:3

45 **KYOTO**

21 MIE

515:728

22 MIYAGI

7:10

164

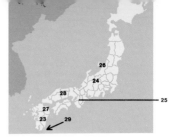

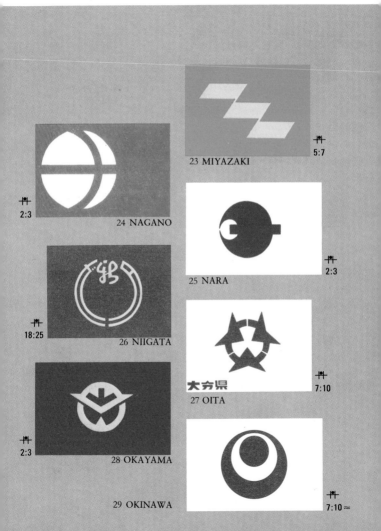

23 MIYAZAKI

5:7

24 NAGANO

2:3

25 NARA

2:3

26 NIIGATA

18:25

27 OITA

大分県

7:10

28 OKAYAMA

2:3

29 OKINAWA

7:10 ≈

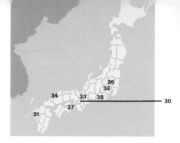

2:3
30 OSAKA

2:3
31 SAGA

2:3
32 SAITAMA

2:3
33 SHIGA

2:3 ≈
34 SHIMANE

2:3
35 SHIZUOKA

2:3 ≈
36 TOCHIGI

徳島県
7:10
37 TOKUSHIMA

166

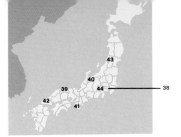

2:3
38 TOKYO

2:3
39 TOTTORI

2:3
40 TOYAMA

2:3
41 WAKAYAMA

2:3
42 YAMAGUCHI

2:3
43 YAMAGATA

7:10
44 YAMANASHI

NORWAY

STATE ARMS

The royal and state arms and the royal flag include the heraldic lion which has characterized Norway since at least 1217. The axe, personal symbol of King/Saint Olav, was added about 1280. The design of the Norwegian national flag corresponds to the crosses found in the Danish and Swedish flags. The colors red, white, ▶ P

Officially approved 17 July 1821; restrictions on use at sea lifted 10 December 1898.

8:11

16:27

ROYAL ARMS

ROYAL FLAG   5:7

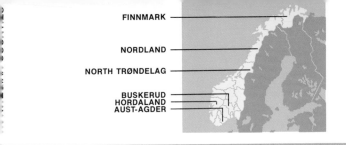

FINNMARK

NORDLAND

NORTH TRØNDELAG

BUSKERUD
HORDALAND
AUST-AGDER

4:5 ≈

AUST [EAST]-AGDER
Officially adopted 12 December 1958.

BUSKERUD
Officially adopted 1 April 1966.

1:1

1:1

FINNMARK
Officially adopted 6 January 1967.

HORDALAND
Officially adopted 1 December 1961.

7:9

1:1

NORD[NORTH]-TRØNDELAG
Officially adopted 8 March 1957.

NORDLAND
Officially adopted 15 January 1965.

1:1

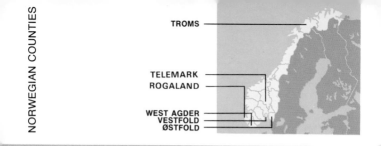

TROMS

TELEMARK
ROGALAND

WEST AGDER
VESTFOLD
ØSTFOLD

1:1

ØSTFOLD
Officially adopted 26 September 1958.

ROGALAND
Officially adopted 11 October 1973.

4:5 ≈

1:1 ≈

TELEMARK
Officially adopted 2 November 1970.

TROMS
Officially adopted 15 January 1960.

1:1 ≈

11:18 ≈

VEST[WEST]-AGDER
Officially adopted 12 December 1958.

VESTFOLD
Officially adopted 30 January 1970.

18:25 ≈

STATE ARMS

The red-white-red shield of Austria goes back to the early thirteenth century, if not before. For centuries, however, it was eclipsed by other symbols when Austria formed part of the Hapsburg dominions in the Austro-Hungarian Empire. As a flag, the red-white-red stripes were first introduced in the war ensign of 1786.

Officially adopted 1 May 1945.

2:3

2:3

Austrian symbols disappeared under Nazi rule from 1938 to 1945; following liberation in that year a broken chain symbolic of regained freedom was added to the eagle's legs.

Different versions bearing royal ciphers or coats of arms were replaced in 1918 by the simple form reestablished after World War II.

The historic Austrian eagle, often represented in the past with two heads, was originally an imperial rather than national symbol. Its lineage can be traced to the Roman Empire.

The sickle, hammer, and civic crown of the eagle stand, respectively, for the peasants, workers, and middle class of modern republican Austria.

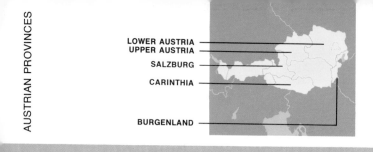

LOWER AUSTRIA
UPPER AUSTRIA
SALZBURG
CARINTHIA

BURGENLAND

++ 2:3 ≈

BURGENLAND
Officially adopted 25 June 1971.

KÄRNTEN
CARINTHIA
Officially adopted 18 June 1946.

++ 2:3 ≈

NIEDERÖSTERREICH
LOWER AUSTRIA
Officially adopted 9 August 1954.

++ 2:3 ≈

OBERÖSTERREICH
UPPER AUSTRIA
Officially adopted 25 April 1949.

++ 2:3 ≈

SALZBURG
Usage initiated 16 February 1921.

++ 2:3 ≈

172

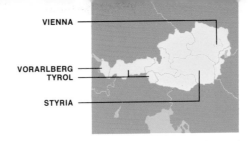

VIENNA

VORARLBERG
TYROL

STYRIA

Without exception, the provincial flags of Austria are based on the principal colors of their arms. This can clearly be seen in the two examples where the plain bicolor (used by private persons) has been modified for use on public buildings by the addition of the arms. A usage common in German-speaking lands is the display of such bicolors in the form of a long vertical "hanging flag."

STEIERMARK
STYRIA
Officially adopted 1960.

⚎ 2:3 ≈

TIROL
TYROL
Usage initiated ca. 25 November 1945.

⚎ 2:3 ≈ ▱

VORARLBERG
Usage initiated ca. 1946.

⚎ 2:3 ≈ ▱

WIEN
VIENNA
Usage initiated ca. 1946.

⚎ 2:3 ≈ ▱

173

STATE ARMS

On 30 December 1906 a flag was raised at Dacca (now in Bangladesh, formerly East Pakistan) when Muslims from all parts of British India gathered. The All-India Muslim League was formed as a result of that meeting, its aim being the achievement of an independent Muslim state. This was realized with the indepen- ▶ P.

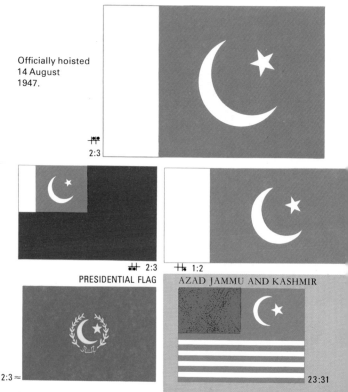

Officially hoisted
14 August
1947.

2:3

2:3
PRESIDENTIAL FLAG

1:2

AZAD JAMMU AND KASHMIR

2:3 ≈

23:31

174

STATE ARMS

The successful revolution which broke out on 3 November 1903 established the flag that has been flown by Panama ever since. It was baptized and officially saluted by civil and military authorities on 20 December of the same year.

The colors chosen corresponded to those used by the two traditional

Officially confirmed 4 June 1904.

2:3 ≈

"For the Benefit of the World" proclaims the motto of Panama, referring to the canal which divides the country physically but provides it with a substantial portion of the national income. The arms incorporate other symbols as well. The civil wars of the past, represented by saber and rifle, have given way to the tools of peaceful labor, promising the prosperity and progress symbolized by the cornucopia and winged wheel. The sun and moon both appear in the central panel of the shield to indicate that independence was achieved at the hour of twilight.

Panamanian political parties—the liberals (red) and conservatives (blue). White was to indicate peace between them, while the orderly division of the field suggested alternation of the parties at the helm of government. Blue and red also were associated with the Atlantic and Pacific oceans, which flank Panama, and with the blood of patriots.

The blue star, according to the flag's designer, stands for the civic virtues of purity and honesty; the red star represents authority and law, which inculcate the former virtues. In the coat of arms there are nine stars corresponding to the provinces into which Panama is divided.

STATE ARMS

To encourage a sense of nationalism among people spread over 600 islands and speaking 700 different languages, it was decided to create national symbols prior to independence.

The committee which toured the country with the proposed designs found some indifference toward its

Officially adopted
11 March 1971;
used at sea
since independence on
16 September 1975.

3:4

STATE ARMS (ALTERNATE)

The arms feature the traditional spear and ceremonial Kundu drum, and a widespread bird of paradise. The use of the name of the country is optional.

proposal for a flag.

A teacher at Catholic Mission High School on Yule Island had asked her art class to draft some flag designs. Susan Karike chose the basic colors red and black because of their extensive use in native art. She added a bird of paradise which provides feathers for traditional dress and ceremonies and had been featured in an unofficial Papua New Guinea flag used at sports events in 1962. The Southern Cross constellation was familiar from the national flag of Australia and reminded Karike of a legend involving five sisters. Her design was presented to the committee when it visited Yule Island, found immediate favor, and was adopted.

STATE ARMS

White, blue, and red flags were used by Paraguayan troops in 1806 when they went to the defense of Buenos Aires during the British invasion. The earliest mention of a red-white-blue tricolor in Paraguay seems to date from 15 August 1812. This bore on one side the arms of the capital city, Asunción, and on the other those of ▶ P. 253

1:2 ≈

Officially adopted 27 November 1842.

TREASURY SEAL

1:2 ≈ NATIONAL FLAG (REVERSE)
1:2 ≈ PRESIDENTIAL FLAG

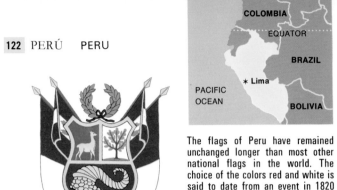

STATE ARMS

The flags of Peru have remained unchanged longer than most other national flags in the world. The choice of the colors red and white is said to date from an event in 1820 when the Argentine leader Captain General José de San Martín arrived to liberate Peru from Spanish domination. He is said to have taken as a

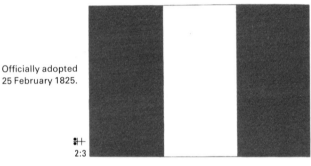

Officially adopted 25 February 1825.

2:3

good omen the flight of a number of flamingos at the time of his arrival; the colors of the birds thereupon became those of the flag of the Peruvian Legion which he founded. Several versions of the flag appeared in the period from 1820 to 1825 when the present form was established.

The shield of the arms is divided into three parts, each representing one of the "kingdoms" over which the Inca Indians considered themselves the master—the animal, vegetable, and mineral. These were symbolized by representative native forms—the vicuña, the cinchona tree, and coins of gold and silver spilling from a cornucopia.

2:3

PRESIDENTIAL FLAG   2:3 ≈

PACIFIC
OCEAN

SOUTH CHINA
SEA

Manila ★

MALAYSIA

STATE ARMS

The present flag was hoisted on 12 June 1898 when the independence of the Philippines was first proclaimed. The red stripe is for courage and bravery, the blue for noble ideals, and white for peace and purity. The three stars symbolize the main geographical areas of the country—Luzon, the Visayas, and Mindanao. The sun

1:2

Officially hoisted 12 June 1898; most recently reestablished 14 October 1943.

26:33

PRESIDENTIAL FLAG

Whenever the Philippines is at war the red stripe is flown at the top of the flag, presumably because red is a symbol of war. At sea any ensign flown upside down is a symbol of distress.

signifies the light of freedom and justice, and its eight rays are for the provinces which first rose in revolt—Manila, Bulacan, Pampanga, Nueva Ecija, Morong, Laguna, Batangas, and Cavite. The triangle is for equality and recalls the Katipunan, which led the revolution. Exact design specifications for the flag were issued on 25 March 1936, following the proclamation of the Commonwealth of the Philippines. The second and third proclamations of Philippine independence came on 14 October 1943 and 4 July 1946, both under the same flag, although usage of that flag had been illegal from 6 September 1907 to 30 October 1919 under the Americans and in 1942 under the Japanese.

STATE ARMS

From the beginning of the thirteenth century the premier emblem associated with Poland has been the White Eagle. Its color and that of the red shield on which it appears have formed the basis for most Polish flags.

Over the centuries many variations of both arms and flags have been dis-

Officially adopted 1 August 1919; reestablished 20 March 1956.

5:8

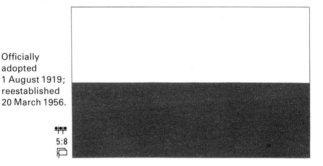

played by Polish ships, military forces, and rulers. In the nineteenth century, when Poland struggled to free itself from foreign domination and to unite the country, the White Eagle and variants of the bicolor based on it were rallying symbols for Polish patriots.

5:8

10:21

5:6

PRESIDENT'S FLAG

STATE ARMS

Alphonso Henry (1112–1185) defeated the Castilians and established Portugal as an independent kingdom. According to the Portuguese national epic, *Os Lusiades,* in 1139 Alphonso also defeated five Moorish kings after they had struck five shields from him in the Battle of Ourique. The divine assistance which aided his victory is

Approved
30 June 1911.

2:3

+|: 12:13

commemorated on each blue shield by five disks, representing the wounds of Christ. These continue to this day as the heart of the Portuguese arms. The armillary sphere—a navigational instrument symbolic of the Age of Discovery when Portuguese sailors opened far parts of the world to European culture and commerce—was the personal symbol of King Manuel I (1495–1521) who had spurred Portuguese exploration. It was added to the Portuguese flag in 1815. The red and green, which replaced blue and white in the flag when Portugal became a republic, recall the historic crosses of Avis and the Order of Christ.

PRESIDENTIAL FLAG   2:3

181

STATE ARMS

The distinctive crimson or maroon characterizing the national symbols of Qatar apparently arose from the effect of the sun on the red natural dyes used in making flags. Because of the similarity of the Qatar flag to those of neighboring states (see Bahrain and the United Arab Emirates), the change was made

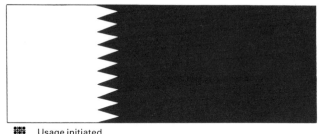

11:28   Usage initiated ca. 1949.

The traditional craft of the Arab sailor, the *dhow*, was used for trading, fishing, and pearl-diving in the area of the Qatar peninsula. The other central emblem of the coat of arms are palm trees, suggesting the oases of the land. The name of the country is written at the top.

The sword has a religious significance: it suggests the dividing edge between right and wrong, between justice and injustice, as well as the militancy of the Islamic faith.

official.

The flag was apparently first used under Shaikh Jasim bin Muhammad al-Thani about 1855. Variations existed over the years, including one in which the name of the country was inscribed in white on the crimson background.

Red is the traditional color of the Kharijite Muslims of eastern Arabia. In the early 19th century Great Britain was instrumental in having borders or stripes of white added to the previously all red flags. The serration between the two colors in the Qatari flag is purely a decorative motif.

182

REPOBLIKA DEMOKRA-
TIKA MALAGASY
MADAGASCAR

STATE ARMS

Many Malagasy are descended from settlers who originally came from Southeast Asia whose red and white flags (see Indonesia) may have influenced similar red and white flags flown by the Hova Empire in 19th century Madagascar. Those Hova flags were the basis for the tricolor adopted shortly after Madagascar

Officially hoisted
21 October
1958.

2:3 ≈

The outer edge of the coat of arms is framed with agricultural products such as rice, while the move to industrialization is symbolized by a cogwheel at the bottom. The rising sun of a new day is surmounted by a rifle, a spade, and a pen. These stand, respectively, for defense of national sovereignty, development of the land, and education. These provide the impetus toward progress represented by the arrowheads above each symbol. The motto at the bottom, below waves suggesting the insular nature of the country, translates as "Fatherland, Revolution, Liberty."

became the Malagasy Republic. Green was added for the coastal peoples.

Historically, red is associated with the Volamena and the white with the Volafotsi, princely families founded by King Andriandahifotsi (1610–1685). His personal emblem was a red bull, and the name of his kingdom was Menabe, "Great Red." Today the white is seen as a symbol of purity, the red of sovereignty, and the green of hope. The arms but not the flag changed when the Second Republic was proclaimed on 30 December 1975.

STATE ARMS

The early 19th century saw the Dominican people struggling for independence—against not only Spain and France, but also the Haitians with whom they share the island of Hispaniola. After several unsuccessful attempts, independence was finally achieved on 27 February 1844 under the banner still in use

Officially confirmed 6 November 1844; reestablished 14 September 1863.

2:3 ≈

2:3 ≈

The motto "God, Fatherland, Liberty" and religious symbols characterize the arms. The blue is said to stand for liberty, red for the fire and blood of the independence struggle. The white cross is a symbol of sacrifice.

today.

The leader of the independence movement was Juan Pablo Duarte, who on 16 July 1838 had formed a secret revolutionary society, the Trinitarian. This name referred to the cells of three individuals who composed the group and also to their religious faith. The faith was asserted in the white cross the Dominicans added to the Haitian flag then flying over the island, which consisted of horizontal stripes of blue over red. Later the Dominican flag was modified to the extent of reversing the position of the blue and red quarters at the fly end of the flag.

STATE ARMS

The flag colors of Romania are heraldic; their origins may be found in ancient banners of Moldavia, Walachia, and Transylvania. One of the earliest combinations of the three colors was created in 1834 by permission of the Ottoman sultan at the request of the Prince of Walachia. As a national symbol, a tricolor of

Officially adopted 21 August 1965.

2:3

FLAG OF THE CHAIRMEN OF THE COUNCILS OF STATE AND OF MINISTERS

1:1

The river, forests, oil derrick, wreath of wheat, and mountains in the coat of arms suggest important natural resources of Romania. The rising sun and star express the promise of a new day under Communism.

blue-yellow-red became firmly established during the revolutionary events of 1848, although official recognition was not given until the union of Walachia and Moldavia in 1859. In subsequent years various governments altered the arms on its center stripe to reflect different ideologies.

After the proclamation of a people's republic in 1947 a completely new coat of arms was decreed. This emblem, bearing a tractor and three furnaces surrounded by a wreath of wheat, was replaced a few months later by a design similar to the one currently in use. Subsequent modifications were made in 1952 and 1965.

185

STATE ARMS

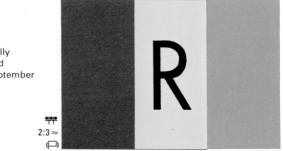

Officially
hoisted
ca. September
1961.

2:3 ≈

The "R" of this banner obviously
represents the name of the country
over which the flag flies. Historically,
it has further associations of equal
importance—revolution, referendum,
and republic.

To free themselves from the feudal
and authoritarian regime of the minority Tutsi clan, the Hutu majority
rose in revolt in November 1959. The
Tutsi king fled and a republic was
proclaimed in January 1961; the new,
democratic political structure was
confirmed in a referendum the following September. The flag hoisted in
January had equal vertical stripes of
red, yellow, and green, but since this
was exactly the same as the flag of
Guinea, an "R" was added after the
September vote.

The red stripe represents blood shed
in the revolution; yellow is for peace,
tranquillity, and liberation from the
tyranny of the past; green is for hope
in the future and the agricultural
wealth of the land.

Under the Tutsi monarchy
Rwanda's highest symbol of state
was Kalinga, the royal drum from
which the king himself supposedly derived authority. The
coat of arms adopted by the
republic displays the flag which
replaced Kalinga as a symbol. It
also includes the name of the
state and its motto—"Liberty,
Cooperation, Progress." A dove
of peace surmounts a bow and
arrow (for defense of democratic
liberties) and the tools of an
agricultural people, a hoe and
pruning knife.

ATLANTIC OCEAN

DOMINICAN REPUBLIC

★ Basseterre

CARIBBEAN SEA

STATE ARMS

Formerly British, the islands of St. Christopher (locally known as St. Kitts), Nevis, and Anguilla became an Associated State on 27 February 1967. Henceforth only foreign and military affairs were handled by Great Britain. At the time of writing (April 1979) negotiations are underway for complete independence and consider-

1:2

Officially hoisted 27 February 1967.

⊹⊢ 1:2

ANGUILLA

⊹⊢ 1:2 ≈ ▱

ation is being given to the adoption of a new national flag.

The three palm fronds in the national flag signify the three islands. They spring from a single trunk, standing for unity, while the roots are for growth. The green, yellow, and blue suggest the vegetation of the islands, the tropical sun, and the waters of the Caribbean. The coat of arms likewise has symbols intended to represent the three constituent islands, their environment, and their history.

Anguilla seceded on 30 May 1967; its flag, still unofficially in use, dates from October 1967. Since 1976 the island, while legally tied to St. Kitts and Nevis, has been under British administration.

ATLANTIC OCEAN

DOMINICAN REPUBLIC

Castries ★

CARIBBEAN SEA

STATE ARMS

Two remarkable geological formations of volcanic origin mark the coast of Saint Lucia—the Pitons. These are represented as the central emblem of the flag; their sheer rise out of the sea toward the sky suggested them as symbols of hope. The black color and the narrow white border reflect the two principal races

1:2

Officially hoisted 22 February 1979.

1:2   GOVERNOR-GENERAL'S FLAG

Information on the post-independence coat of arms was not available at the time of writing. The arms shown above were granted by royal warrant on 16 August 1939. Its Latin motto means "An Anchorage by No Means Unsafe for Ships."

of the island. Gold is for sunshine and blue for the sea in the design, which was created by a local artist, Dunstan St. Omer. The flag was introduced on 1 March 1967 when Saint Lucia became an Associated State. At the time of independence the height of the yellow triangle was increased, but otherwise the flag remained unchanged.

The roses and fleurs-de-lis of the arms are for the British and French rule the island has known, the bamboo suggesting its vegetation. Without its motto, and set on a white disk in the center of the fly-half of a British Blue Ensign, the 1939 arms were the basis for the flag flown by government vessels until 1967.

133 SAINT VINCENT

STATE ARMS

In the 19th century the British colony of Saint Vincent had a seal bearing the Latin motto ''Peace and Justice'' and allegorical figures of two women in classical clothing, presumably representing these virtues. In the late 19th century this was established as a flag badge for government vessels, defacing the fly half of the British

1:2

Officially hoisted as state flag 27 October 1975.

GOVERNOR'S FLAG

In anticipation of April 1979 independence, a new flag has been proposed (of blue-yellow-green vertical stripes and the Saint Vincent arms on a central green breadfruit leaf) but not officially confirmed.

Blue Ensign. On 12 November 1912 it was adapted for use as a coat of arms, its crest being a sprig of cotton.
In 1967 Saint Vincent did not become an Associated State like several other British colonies, although a flag (with horizontal stripes of green-yellow-blue and a central badge) was designed for that eventuality. When associated statehood did go into effect eight years later, no alteration was made in the design of the Saint Vincent Blue Ensign. A postage stamp dating from 1969 showed the full coat of arms in the center of a blue flag—a design which was not in fact ever in use, although it appeared in several books as the Saint Vincent flag.

189

WESTERN SAMOA

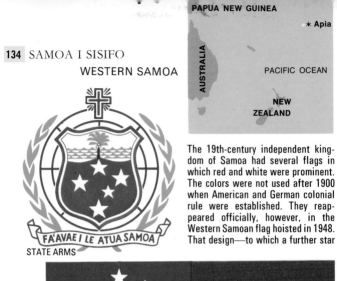

STATE ARMS

1:2
Officially adopted 24 February 1949.

The 19th-century independent kingdom of Samoa had several flags in which red and white were prominent. The colors were not used after 1900 when American and German colonial rule were established. They reappeared officially, however, in the Western Samoan flag hoisted in 1948. That design—to which a further star was added the next year—was created by Their Highnesses Tupua Tamasese Mea'ole and Malietoa Tanumafili II.

Until 1962, when independence was achieved, Western Samoa flew the flag of New Zealand at sea and, jointly with its own flag, on land. Today Western Samoa's sole official flag is honored in the national anthem, *Banner of Freedom*. Its colors are generally associated with courage (red), purity (white), and freedom (blue). Western Samoa, a former U.N. Trust Territory, is the only country whose arms incorporate the seal of the United Nations in its own official arms.

Three symbols of the Christian faith of Samoans are embodied in the national arms. The cross at the top reflects the motto, which is translated as "May God Be the Foundation of Samoa." The constellation of the Southern Cross in the arms (and flag) also suggests Christianity, while linking Western Samoa to other nations. The flag and/or arms of Australia, New Zealand, Brazil, Papua New Guinea, the Falkland Islands, and several Brazilian and Australian states include the same constellation.

190

ADRIATIC
SEA

San Marino ✶

ITALY

MEDIT. SEA

STATE ARMS

According to tradition, this republic was founded in the third century by St. Marinus as a refuge for those fleeing from political or religious persecution: hence the Latin motto ("Liberty") in its arms. The sky is reflected in the blue of the flag and shield; white is for the clouds or the snow that caps Mt. Titano in the

Officially
adopted
6 April 1862.

3:4 ≈

3:4 ≈

winter. The traditional white and blue colors were selected for the cockade of San Marino in 1797. The flag was probably created at the same time, although there is no law regulating its design or usage even today.

The emblem of the three towers surmounted by ostrich plumes goes back at least to the 14th century. They correspond to the three towers of the walled capital city that crowns the mountain which is San Marino's sole territory. These towers—Guaita, Cesta, and Montale—have metal vanes at the top corresponding to the feathers in the arms.

Although San Marino has been a republic for centuries, it has a crown in its arms and flag. This is a symbol of sovereignty (as in the arms of Austria) rather than of monarchy.

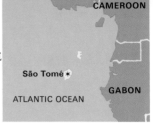

CAMEROON

São Tomé ✳

ATLANTIC OCEAN

GABON

STATE ARMS

The two stars of the national flag are for the country's islands, although it has a unitary rather than federal system of government. The yellow stripe is a symbol of cacao; the vegetation which flourishes on the islands is recalled in the green stripes. The red triangle commemorates the blood of national martyrs,

1:2

Officially adopted 5 November 1975.

shed in the struggle for independence.

After hundreds of years under Portuguese colonial rule, the islands saw their flag hoisted on independence day, 12 July 1975. The organization which had negotiated with the Portuguese for independence was the MLSTP (Movement for the Liberation of São Tomé and Príncipe, originally the Committee for the Liberation of São Tomé and Príncipe). Its Political Bureau designed the flag. The colors of the flag are the same as those found in other former Portuguese colonies in Africa—Mozambique, Cape Verde, and Guinea-Bissau—as well as a number of other African nations.

Native birds of the two islands for which the country is named flank the shield in the arms of São Tomé and Príncipe. The name of the country is represented in the national language, Portuguese, on the top ribbon while the national motto—"Unity, Discipline, Work"—is inscribed on the bottom ribbon. The tree in the arms recall that cocoa and copra are the chief crops and income source of the nation.

STATE ARMS

ATLANTIC OCEAN

MAURITANIA

★ Dakar

MALI

GUINEA-BISSAU

GUINEA

As France divested itself of its colonies in the late 1950s, new leaders—including Léopold Sédar Senghor of Senegal, whose initials appear today on the flag he displays as president of his nation—called for the unity of Africa. Senegal and the French Sudan established the Mali Federation in early 1959; it achieved

Officially adopted September 1960.

2:3 ≈

3:4 ≈ PRESIDENTIAL FLAG

independence on 20 June 1960. Its flag had vertical stripes of green-yellow-red, the center stripe bearing in black the figure of a man. Then two months later Senegal broke from the young federation and became independent. The symbol of the man was replaced with a green star, later incorporated into Senegal's coat of arms.

The equal vertical stripes were undoubtedly inspired by those of the French Tricolor. The flag colors were found in Senegalese political party flags, but their extensive usage has caused them to be recognized as general pan-African colors.

The arms bear a lion, symbol of strength; the Senegal River, which forms the nation's northern border; and the native baobab tree. The national motto is "One People, One Aim, One Faith."

STATE ARMS

Red in the national flag of Seychelles is seen as a symbol of progress and revolution, green signifying both the land and the reliance of the people on agriculture. The white wavy band is to recall waves along the beaches and the resources of the Indian Ocean. Originally, when it was used by the Seychelles People's United Party, the

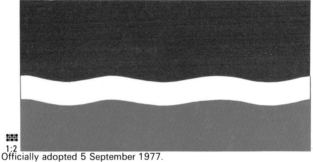

1:2

Officially adopted 5 September 1977.

1:2   PRESIDENTIAL FLAG

No color representation of the Seychelles arms being available, the above is colored after the flag badge the islands used prior to independence and the official heraldic description of the arms.

flag had a rising yellow sun, but this has been omitted, to indicate that the sun of liberation has finally dawned over the nation. The flag was brought into use on 26 June 1977, following the revolution on the fifth of that month.

The coat of arms has elements dating back to the 19th century. General Charles "Chinese" Gordon chose the tortoise, coco-de-mer palm tree, and the Latin motto which proclaims "The End Crowns the Work." After use in two different versions as a flag badge for Seychelles as a British colony, it became the basis for the arms established at the time of independence in 1976. Sailfish serve as supporters, while a white-tailed tropical bird appears in the crest.

STATE ARMS

A century ago the black, double-headed eagle represented imperial Austria-Hungary, Russia, and the past glories of the Byzantine Empire. Its use by the Albanian national hero, George Castriota (known as Iskander Beg or Skanderbeg), was not entirely forgotten, however. When modern Albania became independent in 1912,

Officially
confirmed
15 March 1946.

5:7

2:3 ≈ ▯

2:3

the nation resurrected Skanderbeg's red flag with the double-headed eagle.

Since that time many symbols have accompanied the eagle on the flag—a star of independence, crown of royalty, fasces of Italian domination, and gold-bordered red star of Communism.

The Albanian war ensign is modeled on that of the Soviet Union—a stripe along the bottom edge of a white field bearing national symbols. The star and red ribbon of the arms proclaim the Communist philosophy of the state. The date heralds the National Anti-Fascist Congress of Liberation held in Permet.

STATE ARMS

Sierra Leone has one of the few hilly areas on the West African coast; hence, green mountains were incorporated into its coat of arms. The green stripe in its flag symbolizes agriculture and natural resources as well as the mountains.

The blue in both the arms and the flag recall that the capital city, Freetown,

Officially hoisted 27 April 1961.

2:3

The technical heraldic description of the Sierra Leone arms is as follows: "Vert [green] on a Base Barry wavy of four [stripes] Argent and Azure [white and blue] a Lion passant Or [gold] on a Chief dancetty of three points also Argent as many Torches Sable [black] enflamed proper [of natural color]. And for the Supporters: On either side a Lion Or supporting between the fore legs an Oil-palm proper: together with this Motto Unity Freedom Justice."

has one of the best natural harbors on the African coast. The color stands for the hope that the nation may be able to make a contribution to world peace in the development of commerce through this harbor. The white stripe that separates the "cobalt blue" and "leaf green" in the state flag is an emblem of unity and justice. The lion of the arms refers to the national name and links Sierra Leone with its former colonial master, Great Britain. Pride in the education its university colleges have provided to West Africa is evidenced in the flaming torches of enlightenment in the national arms.

STATE ARMS

SOUTH
CHINA SEA

MALAYSIA

★ **Singapore**

INDONESIA

The national motto—"Forward
Singapore"—is also the title of the
national anthem. The tiger in the arms
recalls former association with
Malaysia and the other supporter
brings to mind the meaning of the
name Singapore—"Lion City." A
lion represented Singapore in the
arms of the Straits Settlements gran- ▶ P. 253

Officially hoisted
3 December 1959.

2:3

1:2

1:2

1:2

1:2 PRESIDENTIAL FLAG

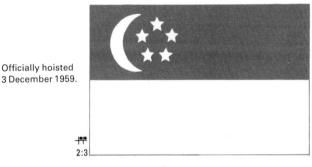

STATE ARMS

A number of flag designs were debated in the Legislative Assembly prior to the independence of the Solomon Islands. Many of the symbols contained in these proposals were eventually incorporated in the flag which became official eight months prior to independence. The stars correspond to the five districts— ▶ P

1:2

Officially adopted 18 November 1977.

⊣⊢ 1:2

⊢⊢ 1:2

⊣⊢ 1:2

-1:2   GOVERNOR-GENERAL'S FLAG

143 SOOMAALIYA
SOMALIA

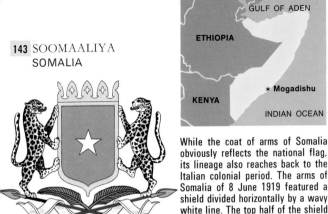

STATE ARMS

While the coat of arms of Somalia obviously reflects the national flag, its lineage also reaches back to the Italian colonial period. The arms of Somalia of 8 June 1919 featured a shield divided horizontally by a wavy white line. The top half of the shield was blue with a leopard in natural color surmounted by a white five-

Officially hoisted
12 October
1954.

2:3 ≈

pointed star. The present arms were adopted on 10 October 1956.

Although bound by religion, ethnic ties, language, and history, the Somalis were divided in the 19th century by the British, French, and Italians. The largest part of the territory became an Italian colony which achieved independence on 30 June 1960. Its flag had been hoisted on 26 June 1960 in the former colony of British Somaliland, which united four days later with its neighbor to the south.

While the star and colors of the flag may have been suggested by the use of those symbols in the Somali arms, they are generally related to the blue and white of the United Nations flag.

The five points of the star refer to the areas in which Somalis live. In addition to the former Italian and British colonies, this includes the Ogaden region of Ethiopia, the Northern Frontier District of Kenya, and Djibouti.

The irredentist claim implicit in this star is not unique. Bolivia adopted its war ensign in 1966 to press its claim to the littoral which it had lost in a war with Chile in 1879. For centuries the arms of England included the arms of France because the sovereigns of the former claimed title to the latter.

199

144 SOUTH AFRICA/ SUID AFRIKA

STATE ARMS

Two British colonies (Natal and the Cape) and two formerly independent Boer states (the Orange Free State and the South African Republic) united to form South Africa. It was decided to combine the flags of the latter two with the Union Jack of the former as a special badge. This was added to the orange-white-blue flag

Officially hoisted 31 May 1928.

2:3

2:3

PRESIDENT'S FLAG

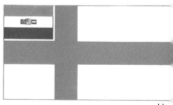

PRIME MINISTER'S FLAG

2:3

GAZANKULU

TRANSVAAL

ORANGE FREE STATE

THE CISKEI

originally brought to South Africa by Dutch settlers in the seventeenth century.

Until 1951 this flag was only flown on land, and until 1957 it was always officially flown on public buildings jointly with the Union Jack. No change was made in the flag when South Africa became a republic in 1961.

The coat of arms has two official artistic versions (as seen, for example, in the flags of the president and prime minister). The lion crest recalls both English and Dutch use of this symbol. The lion also reinforces the national motto, "Strength from Unity."

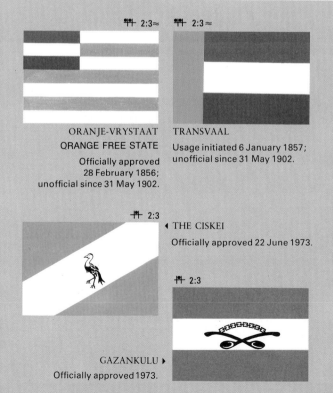

⚓ 2:3 ≈

ORANJE-VRYSTAAT
ORANGE FREE STATE

Officially approved
28 February 1856;
unofficial since 31 May 1902.

⚓ 2:3 ≈

TRANSVAAL

Usage initiated 6 January 1857;
unofficial since 31 May 1902.

⚓ 2:3

◀ THE CISKEI

Officially approved 22 June 1973.

⚓ 2:3

GAZANKULU ▶
Officially approved 1973.

201

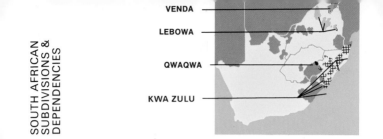

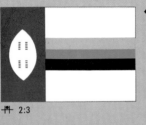

◀ KWA ZULU
Officially approved 1977.

⚓ 2:3

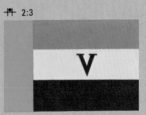

LEBOWA ▲
Officially approved 5 July 1974.

⚓ 2:3

⚓ 2:3   ▲ QWAQWA
Officially adopted 18 July 1975.

VENDA ▶
Officially approved 1973.

The ruling European minority in South Africa has created "native homelands" of which South African blacks are considered citizens. Among the limited rights of self-government of these territories are use of a flag (flown subordinate to the South African national flag), a parliamentary mace, a coat of arms, and an anthem. Independence has been granted to two homelands, Transkei and Bophuthatswana.

202

STATE ARMS

The Red Banner was well established
as a symbol of revolution at the time
the Bolsheviks seized control of what
is today Leningrad, organizing the
first Soviet state. On 14 April 1918,
they added the inscription *Russian
Socialist Federative Soviet Republic*
in gold in the upper hoist. In July the
new constitution allowed the option

1:2

Officially adopted 19 August 1955.

+‡ 3:5

+‡ 2:3 ⌶

of inscribing the abbreviation РСФСР
(RSFSR in Cyrillic) instead of the
name, and in 1920 this was given a
precise artistic form.

While that flag continued in use until
1954, Soviet Russia united with other
Communist states in 1922 to form the
Soviet Union. The original concept for
a USSR flag showed the coat of arms
on a red field. Instead, it was decided
to use the hammer and sickle (symbols of the proletariat and peasantry)
and the five-pointed star which
stands for the unity of peoples in all
five continents. That proposal was
made on 12 November 1923 and
became official on 31 January 1924 in
its original artistic rendition, since
altered.

203

UNION REPUBLICS OF THE U.S.S.R.

KAZAKH S.S.R.
ESTONIAN S.S.R.
LATVIAN S.S.R.
LITHUANIAN S.S.R.
BYELORUSSIAN S.S.R.

ARMENIAN S.S.R.
AZERBAIDZHAN S.S.R.

KIRGIZ S.S.R.

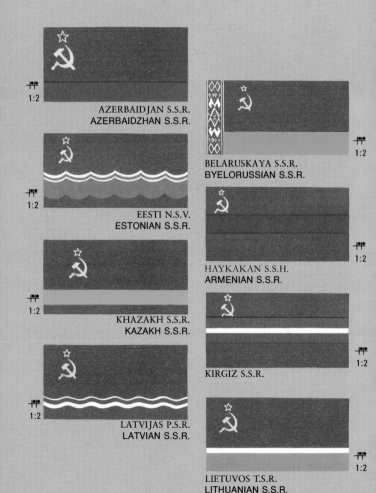

AZERBAIDJAN S.S.R.
AZERBAIDZHAN S.S.R.

EESTI N.S.V.
ESTONIAN S.S.R.

KHAZAKH S.S.R.
KAZAKH S.S.R.

LATVIJAS P.S.R.
LATVIAN S.S.R.

BELARUSKAYA S.S.R.
BYELORUSSIAN S.S.R.

HAYKAKAN S.S.H.
ARMENIAN S.S.R.

KIRGIZ S.S.R.

LIETUVOS T.S.R.
LITHUANIAN S.S.R.

204

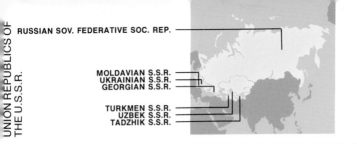

RUSSIAN SOV. FEDERATIVE SOC. REP.

MOLDAVIAN S.S.R.
UKRAINIAN S.S.R.
GEORGIAN S.S.R.

TURKMEN S.S.R.
UZBEK S.S.R.
TADZHIK S.S.R.

1:2

R.S.S. MOLDOVENESHT
MOLDAVIAN S.S.R.

1:2

ROSSIISKAYA S.F.S.R.
RUSSIAN SOV. FED. SOC. REP.

1:2

TURKMENISTAN S.S.R.
TURKMEN S.S.R.

1:2

UZBEKISTAN S.S.R.
UZBEK S.S.R.

1:2

R.S.S. TADJIKISTAN
TADZHIK S.S.R.

1:2

SAKHARTVELOS S.S.R.
GEORGIAN S.S.R.

1:2

UKRAINS'KA R.S.R.
UKRAINIAN S.S.R.

Until the early 1950s the flags of
the constituent Union Republics
were of a common pattern
consisting of a red field, a
hammer-sickle-star emblem in
gold, and the initials of the state
in gold.

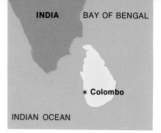

INDIA   BAY OF BENGAL

* Colombo

INDIAN OCEAN

STATE ARMS

Legend credits Prince Vijaya, Aryan conqueror of Ceylon in the sixth century B.C., with descent from a lion. Ancient Singhalese royal palaces feature carved lions and a 15th century saga refers to a lion banner.
The flag of the last king of Kandy (later Ceylon and later still, Sri Lanka) was returned to Britain as war booty

Officially hoisted 7 September 1978.

5:9 ≈

+ 3:5 ≈

In the Sri Lanka arms the pot of rice is a symbol of prosperity; the sun and moon are for longevity as in the Nepal flag. At the top is a representation of the Buddhist Wheel of the Law, also found in the flag of India.

in 1815. Upon the restitution of Ceylonese independence in 1948, a replica of this banner was hoisted as the national flag, but three years later stripes of orange and green were added. These represented the Hindu and Muslim minorities, the Tamils and Moors.
The bo leaves of the sacred pipul tree in the corners are a symbol of the religion of the majority. Gautama is supposed to have received enlightenment, becoming the Buddha after meditation under a pipul tree. Another Buddhist symbol, the lotus, surrounds the national lion and sword in the center of the coat of arms.

STATE ARMS

The flag chosen after the revolution of 1969 was designed by a Khartoum Art Institute graduate, Abdalrahman Ahmad Aljali. It is based on the Arab Liberation Flag (see Egypt). Red is seen as the color of revolution, progress, socialism, and national martyrs. White is for peace, optimism, and light; it also recalls the white flag

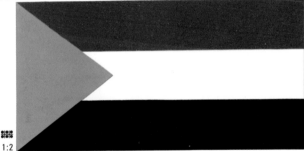

1:2

Officially hoisted 20 May 1970.

≈ 🏳 PRESIDENTIAL FLAG

flown in the 1924 revolution. Green is hailed as a symbol of prosperity and Islam. Sudan is an Arabic word meaning "black" and the country is partly in black Africa. Moreover, one of the flags of the Madhi, a 19th century Sudanese leader, was black.

BAHR EL GHAZAL   ┼╫┼ 2:3 ≈   ┼╫┼ 2:3 ≈
NORTHERN KORDOFAN

NORWEGIAN SEA

U.S.S.R.

NORWAY

SWEDEN

Helsinki ∗

The flag of Finland originated in the 19th century. At that time Finland was part of Russia, although it had limited autonomy. Many Finns seeking to create a distinctive local flag looked for inspiration to their national coat of arms, which dates back to at least 1557. Its red shield and gold lion provided the basic colors for many ▶ P. 25

STATES ARMS

Officially adopted 12 February 1920.

11:18

11:18

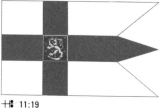

11:19

ÅLAND   17:26

11:19   PRESIDENTIAL FLAG

149 SURINAME

STATE ARMS

The star is for unity (as in many other national flags), while its yellow color stands for sacrifice, the golden future, and the self-confidence and altruism the people require in working for national progress. Red is seen as symbolic of love and a progressive spirit, while white symbolizes justice and freedom. The verdure which

Officially hoisted 25 November 1975.

2:3

PRESIDENTIAL FLAG 2:3
PRIME MINISTER'S FLAG

2:3

covers the nation and the hope for progress are incarnated in the green stripes.

In contrast to the flag the arms are quite old. While there have been modifications over the years, the basic design dates to the 17th century. The Amerindians were the original inhabitants of Suriname and many still live in rural areas. The ship, central diamond, and tree in the arms speak of the commerce, mining, and agriculture of the land. The Latin motto translated is "Justice, Piety, Faith." The arms in their present form date from 15 December 1959, except that at the time of independence the color of the hair of the Amerindians was altered to black.

STATE ARMS

Following World War II, when most independent Arab states were monarchies, Syria had a republican form of government. The coat of arms Syria adopted at that time seems to have influenced the designing of later Arab republican coats of arms.

The central feature of the Syrian arms was the eagle emblem of General

Officially hoisted
1 January 1972.

2:3

In September 1971 Syria joined Libya and Egypt in the Federation of Arab Republics whose new flag and arms were established on the first day of the following year. From 1963 to 1972 Syria had used a flag of the same three colors, but with three green stars on the white stripe. A similar design constituted the Syrian flag from 1932 to 1958 and from 1961 to 1963. From 1958 to 1961 Syria joined Egypt in the United Arab Republic under a red-white-black tricolor bearing two green stars. Syria is currently (April 1979) planning to unify with Iraq.

Khalid ibn al-Walid, Muslim conqueror of Damascus in the seventh century. The central shield bore the stars and colors of the Syrian flag; below were the wreath and ribbon with the name of the state.

The arms created in late 1971 for the Federation of Arab Republics shows a hawk, emblem of the Quraish tribe to which Muhammad belonged, but the artistic rendition is very similar to the original Syrian eagle. The shield is now plain and the ribbon bears the inscription ''Federation of Arab Republics.'' The Syrian and Egyptian national flags are exactly the same.

GREATER STATE ARMS

The lesser arms of Sweden, associated with the country rather than its ruling dynasty, date from 1364 when they appear on a seal employed by King Albrekt. Varying interpretations have been given to the three crowns. In the greater state arms they appear quartered with the dynastic arms of the Folkung kings who ruled ▶ P. 254

Officially adopted 22 June 1906.

5:8

LESSER STATE ARMS

ROYAL COMMAND FLAG

1:1

ROYAL FLAG

1:2

1:2

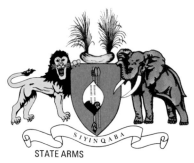

STATE ARMS

The Swazi Pioneer Corps which served with the British during World War II received their standard from King Sobhuza II in 1941 as a reminder of Swazi military traditions. More than a quarter-century later, when Swaziland's independence from Britain was imminent, the corps color provided the basis for the design of

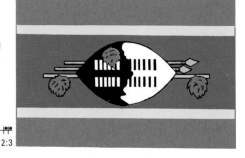

Officially hoisted 30 October 1967.

2:3

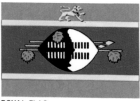

ROYAL FLAG   2:3

The lion and elephant stand for the king and queen mother: the motto, which refers to them, means "We Are the Fortress." The royal headdress with its widow bird feathers serves as a crest to the shield in the national arms.

the national flag. The new pattern, introduced on 25 April 1967, took its present form five months later.

Independence within the British Commonwealth was achieved on 6 September 1968. The following year the king, then in the 47th year of his reign, designed his own royal standard by adding his personal emblem (a lion) to the national flag.

The crimson in the flags is for the battles of the past, yellow for the wealth of mineral resources, and blue for peace. The shield reflects natural oxhide colors; the spears and staff bear feathers of the widow bird and lourie.

212

153 TANZANIA

STATE ARMS

The flag of the Tanganyika African National Union (TANU) heralded the nation's fertile land by two horizontal stripes of green, separated by a black stripe to indicate the ethnic majority of the population. On 9 December 1961, when Tanganyika became independent, a national flag was hoisted: gold fimbriations were added to

Officially approved ca. 30 June 1964.

2:3≈

PRESIDENTIAL FLAG

ZANZIBAR

2:3

stand for Tanganyika's mineral resources.

After neighboring Zanzibar was amalgamated in 1964, the general form of the Tanganyikan flag was retained by Tanzania but in a diagonal rather than horizontal pattern. The introduction of blue reflected the flag of Zanzibar and the Indian Ocean.

The Swahili motto ''Freedom and Unity'' frames Mount Kilimanjaro in the Tanzanian arms. Among other symbols are found tools of development (an ax and hoe), a spear for defense, the flaming torch of freedom and knowledge, and leading agricultural resources (cotton and cloves).

213

STATE ARMS

Like some of the other former French colonies, Chad looked to the French Tricolor in creating its own national flag. Here the pan-African colors (green, yellow, and red) have been slightly altered in order that the flag not conflict with those of neighboring countries. The blue stripe has been officially described as a symbol of the

Officially
adopted
6 November
1959.

2:3

In the early days of heraldry, a coat of arms was one of the most personal possessions of an individual. Because a king and the area he ruled were intimately associated, his personal arms came to be considered as the state emblem—a situation that still exists in a few countries. In sharp contrast is the usage of coats of arms today, exemplified by the arms of Chad. Designed by foreigners and appearing largely on postage stamps and medals made expressly for sale to foreigners, the coat of arms is scarcely ever seen within Chad itself.

sky, hope, agriculture, and the southern part of the country. Yellow is seen as a symbol of both the northern (desert) half of the country and the sun. Red stands for progress, unity, and the willingness of citizens to sacrifice themselves for the country. The national coat of arms, designed by two Frenchmen in 1970, is in the European style. The national motto ("Unity, Work, Progress") appears on a ribbon at the bottom below a representation of the national order with its ribbon. The importance of coats of arms in former French colonies like Chad is slight, especially since France itself has long lacked official arms.

STATE ARMS

The green stripes in the Togo flag have a double symbolism—hope for the future and the agricultural work of the people on which that hope is founded. The yellow stripes indicate a faith in work as the basis of the moral and material well-being of the nation. The white star, an emblem of purity, is said to be a reminder to all citizens

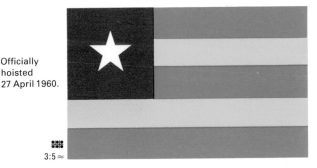

Officially hoisted 27 April 1960.

3:5 ≈

The uniformity in all aspects of government introduced by French revolutionaries in the late 18th century is seen in nations once under French control or influence. In Togo, Benin, Mali, the Ivory Coast, and elsewhere there is a single flag employed for all purposes—private, public, and military display both on land and at sea. Visually, the usage of one flag instead of many reinforces the concepts of national unity and the responsibility of the central government for the ordering of the society.

that they must show themselves worthy of their nation's independence. The red of the canton is officially described as "the color of charity, of fidelity, of love, of those cardinal virtues which inspire love of fellow humans and the sacrifice of one's life—if necessary—for the triumph of the principles of humanity and the pushing back of the frontiers of human misery." Lions in the Togo arms reflect the courage of the people. The bows and arrows call on all citizens to be active in defense of the liberties of the country. The national motto inscribed at the top of the arms translates as "Work, Liberty, Fatherland."

ROYAL ARMS

The importance of Christianity, introduced into Tonga in the early nineteenth century, is underscored by the national and royal flags and royal arms.

In the first parliament of the nation, held in 1862, King George Tupou I called for suggestions for a national flag. After much discussion he put

1:2

Officially confirmed 4 November 1875.

ROYAL FLAG

26:37

The stars in the royal flag stand for the main island groups united in Tonga—Tongatapu, Ha'apai, and Vava'u. The motto, chosen by King George Tupou I in 1862, reads "God and Tonga Are My Inheritance."

forth his own concept in words tradition preserves thus: "It is my wish that our flag should have the cross of Jesus ... and the flag should be red in color to represent the blood shed on the Cross for our salvation." The actual forms of the flags and arms are credited both to Prince Uelingatoni Ngu Tupoumalohi and to Rev. Shirley Baker, a Wesleyan minister.

The 1875 constitution states that "the Flag of Tonga (the flag of King George) shall never be altered." Christianity's dove of peace in the royal banner holds a myrtle leaf, emblem of national unity.

NAMIBIA
BOTSWANA
SOUTH AFRICA
Umtata *
ATLANTIC OCEAN
INDIAN OCEAN

STATE ARMS

The national flag, flown subordinate to the national flag of South Africa until independence was proclaimed on 26 October 1976, and the coat of arms of Transkei (established on 15 January 1971) feature a distinctive color, ochre. It recalls the local soil, of which one type is used for protection against the sun and as a cos-

Officially adopted
May 1966.

2:3

PRIME MINISTER'S FLAG

Transkei belongs to no international organization and is recognized as an independent state only by Bophuthatswana and South Africa. It has broken diplomatic relations with the latter over territorial claims.

metic, the other as a dye for clothing. It symbolizes protection and self-realization. Green stands for the vegetation of Transkei, and white has been associated with peace and Christianity.

In the arms the chevron symbolizes strength and support. The bull has both religious and economic significance for the Xhosa people of Transkei. The basket, used for grinding corn (the agricultural mainstay), is a token of prosperity. The cogwheel is seen to stand for growth and development through science and technology. Leopard skins are traditionally worn by leaders as a symbol of authority. The national motto, like South Africa's, means "Unity Is Strength."

TOBAGO

★ Port-of-Spain

ATLANTIC OCEAN

VENEZUELA

STATE ARMS

Several interpretations have been given to the colors combined in the arms and flag of this land. Red is said to express the vitality of the land and its peoples, the warmth and energy of the sun, and courage and friendliness. White is a symbol of the sea, of the purity of national aspirations, and the equality of all men. Black is seen as

Officially hoisted 31 August 1962.

3:5

an emblem of strength, unity, and purpose—as well as the wealth of the land.

Included in the arms are a scarlet ibis, a cocrico, and two hummingbirds— plus the three ships of Christopher Columbus.

1:2

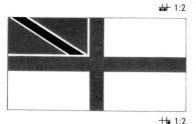
1:2

PRIME MINISTER'S FLAG

3:5≈

STATE ARMS

Usage initiated
ca. 1835.

2:3

PRESIDENTIAL FLAG

1:1 ≈

In the early 19th century Tunisia flew flags of plain red and ones consisting of red and white or red and yellow stripes. Similar flags were flown in other North African countries.

Although nominally under Turkish rule since the 16th century, Tunisia had considerable local autonomy in the early 1800s. This was expressed in the adoption by Hussain II, Bey of Tunis, of a flag slightly different from that of Turkey.

The new flag was distinctive enough to warrant official inquiries by the sultan in Istanbul. These were never answered by the bey and Tunisia's flag did not change. Even later, under French rule and following the abolition of the beylical dynasty, the flag stood unmodified.

Both the Tunisian national coat of arms and presidential standard incorporate the traditional Muslim star and crescent. The coat of arms also has the national motto—"Order, Freedom, Justice"—and symbols characterizing those words (a lion, a ship, and scales). The vessel recalls the earliest settlers in the area, who arrived from Phoenicia, and the modern maritime interests of the nation.

STATE ARMS

The basic form of the national flag was apparently established in 1793 under Sultan Selim III, when the green flags used by the navy were changed to red and a white crescent and multi-pointed star were added. The five-pointed star dates from approximately 1844. Except for the issuance of design specifications, no change

Officially
confirmed
5 June 1936.

2:3

PRESIDENTIAL FLAG

1:1

Red has been prominent in Turkish flags for 700 years. The star and crescent are Muslim symbols, but also have a long pre-Islamic past in Asia Minor.

was made when the Ottoman Empire became the Republic of Turkey and the caliphate (religious authority) was terminated.

Many traditions explain the star and crescent symbol. It is known that Diana was the patron goddess of Byzantium and that her symbol was a moon. In A.D. 330 the Emperor Constantine rededicated the city—which he called Constantinople—to the Virgin Mary, whose star symbol was superimposed over the crescent. In 1453 Constantinople was captured by the Ottoman Turks and renamed Istanbul, but its new rulers may have adopted the existing emblem for their own use.

STATE ARMS

The nine islands which form the nation—Funafuti, Nui, Nanumea, Nukufetau, Niutao, Nukulailai, Nanumanga, Vaitupu, and Nuilakita—and the Pacific Ocean are symbolized by the stars and blue field of the national flag. The Union Jack indicates the close ties which Tuvalu still has with Britain after 86 years of colonial rule.

*Funafuti

AUSTRALIA

PACIFIC OCEAN

NEW ZEALAND

Officially hoisted 1 October 1978.

GOVERNOR-GENERAL'S FLAG   1:2

The name of the country means "eight islands." The ninth island, Nurakita (or Nuilakita), represented by a star on the flag, is uninhabited.

It also associates the flag with others in the Pacific—Australia, New Zealand, Niue, Fiji, the Cook Islands, and Hawaii.

The coat of arms served as a badge in the state ensign of Tuvalu prior to independence and following separation from the former Gilbert and Ellice Islands Colony. The border has banana leaves suggesting the fertility of the island and seashells for the eight inhabited islands. The *Maneapa* or traditional meeting house and the ocean are the central symbols of the arms granted on 3 December 1976. The motto means "Tuvalu for God." The design of the arms was developed by Mr. R.P. Turner, the flag by Mr. Vione Natano.

221

STATE ARMS

The crested crane, not having been employed as the emblem of any kingdoms or tribes of Uganda, could therefore serve as a neutral national symbol. It first appeared in the colonial badge of Uganda under British rule.

The original proposal for the national flag was replaced in May of 1962 by a

Officially hoisted 9 October 1962.

2:3 ≈

PRESIDENTIAL FLAG

1:2 ≈ 🏳

design based on the black-yellow-red flag of the Uganda People's Congress, the party which had just won a national election. The three colors were interpreted to symbolize the people of Africa, sunshine, and brotherhood. The design was suggested by the minister of justice, Mr. Grace Ibingira.

The drum, an important political symbol among traditional intralacustrine East African kingdoms, was incorporated in the flags of three Ugandan kingdoms before the abolition of flags and kingdoms in 1966.

Stylized heraldic waters at the top of the national shield are for the lakes and rivers of Uganda; those which flow beneath it indicate Lake Victoria, source of the White Nile.

STATE ARMS

The Kharijite ("secessionist") Muslims of eastern Arabia adopted the color red centuries ago. Even in the 20th century ships from Oman flew a plain red flag as they sailed throughout the Indian Ocean. In 1970 the British protectorate was terminated and the national flag was "modernized." The state arms—

Officially adopted 17 December 1970.

2:3

++ 2:3 ≈

The national arms in gold surmounted by a crown appear on a green-bordered red square in the center of the red flag which serves as the personal banner of the ruling sultan.

supposedly dating back to the middle of the 18th century—were added in the upper hoist. The crossed swords and dagger of the arms are traditional weapons among the Omani people. The broad stripes of white and green were added to symbolize, respectively, peace and fertility. Historically, white had been associated with the imam, religious leader of Oman and at times a political rival to the ruling sultan. Green traditionally was associated with the Djebel al Akhdar (Green Mountains) and with the Hadji, those who had made the pilgrimage to Mecca.

ATLANTIC OCEAN

NORTH SEA

IRELAND

London ✳

ENGLISH CHANNEL   FRANCE

ROYAL ARMS

The Union Jack is a combination of the crosses of the patron saints of England, Scotland, and Ireland—Saints George, Andrew, and Patrick, respectively. These continue unofficially as their national flags although only the flag of St. Andrew is actually used to any extent. The Union Jack itself is one of the best-known

1:2

Officially hoisted 1 January 1801.

1:2 (🏳)   ROYAL FLAG

QUEEN'S PERSONAL FLAG

1:1

flags in the world because of its striking graphic design, its influence on other flags, and the importance of the British Empire (later Commonwealth) in world history.

The first certain reference in England to the flag of St. George dates from 1277; he became patron of the Order of the Garter in 1348. The primacy of St. Andrew's white saltire in Scotland seems to have been achieved earlier, although the blue background did not become firmly established until the 17th century. The earliest reference to this cross (in the 12th century) imputes an origin going back to King Hungus in the eighth century. The red saltire on white of St. Patrick may well be a 16th century invention,

+ 1:2

++ 2:3 ≈

based on the similar Cross of Burgundy used by the Spaniards. Its use is probably due to the fact that it more conveniently fits in the Union Jack than the arms of Ireland, a gold harp on blue.

The original Union Jack (without St. Patrick's cross) was established by King James VI of Scotland who, upon the death of Queen Elizabeth I in 1603, became King James I of England and united the two kingdoms in his person. When England and Scotland became Great Britain in 1707, the Union Jack was introduced into the ensigns of red, blue, and white which had had the cross of one or the other nation as a canton. The former two have been the basis for over a hundred colonial and national flags of Commonwealth countries (see Canada and New Zealand).

The flag popularly known as the "royal standard," which heraldists refer to as the "royal banner," is composed of the quartered arms of England, Scotland, and Ireland. The sovereign is also entitled to fly a number of other flags. In Commonwealth countries which have a republican form of government, for example, the queen displays a "personal flag." Its central emblem is featured in the special royal flags she employs in the titular monarchies of the Commonwealth (see Australia, Canada, New Zealand, and Jamaica).

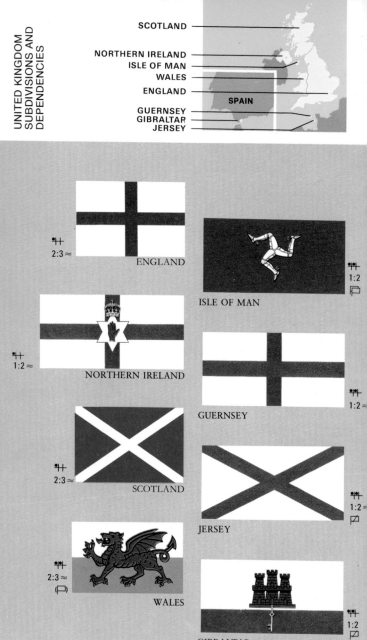

UNITED KINGDOM
SUBDIVISIONS AND
DEPENDENCIES

SCOTLAND

NORTHERN IRELAND
ISLE OF MAN
WALES
ENGLAND   SPAIN

GUERNSEY
GIBRALTAR
JERSEY

ENGLAND

ISLE OF MAN

NORTHERN IRELAND

GUERNSEY

SCOTLAND

JERSEY

WALES

GIBRALTAR

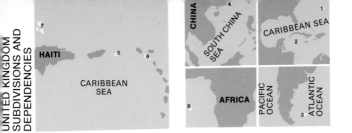

1 BERMUDA

2 CAYMAN ISLANDS

3 FALKLAND ISLANDS

4 HONG KONG

5 BRITISH VIRGIN ISLANDS

6 MONTSERRAT

7 TURKS AND CAICOS ISLANDS

8 ST. HELENA

227

STATE ARMS

When the first truly national American flag (known as the Continental Colors) was decided upon, apparently in December 1775, its canton bore the Union Jack, symbol of Great Britain. The 13 red and white stripes of the field were symbolic of the colonies united in defense of their liberties. It was not until almost a year after the

10:19
Officially hoisted 4 July 1960.

PRESIDENTIAL FLAG   26:33

The eagle of Rome, originally a symbol of the republic, inspired Americans to choose their native bald eagle for the national arms of the new United States in 1782, a design now popular in American heraldry.

Declaration of Independence on 4 July 1776 that Americans finally replaced the Union Jack with what the law of 14 June 1777 refers to as a ''Union [of] 13 stars white in a blue field representing a new constellation.'' Stripes were a common device in the flags of that era, and may have been chosen simply to distinguish the flag from the British Red Ensign. The stars on the other hand are clearly an American invention, and the Stars and Stripes is the first national flag to make use of this geometric symbol, now widespread throughout the world. A concept less widely copied elsewhere is the American system of altering the flag to reflect changes in the number of constituent parts of the ▶ P. 2

The information provided for
each state is, sequentially: (1) the
dates when the states ratified the
Constitution (*) or joined the
Union; (2) in what order; and (3)
when their flags were adopted.

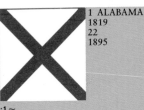

1 ALABAMA
1819
22
1895

1:1 ≈

2 ALASKA   1959   49   1927

125:177

3 ARIZONA   1912   48   1917

2:3

4 ARKANSAS   1836   25   1924

2:3 ≈

5 CALIFORNIA   1850   31   1911

2:3

6 COLORADO   1876   38   1964

2:3

7 CONNECTICUT   1788*   5   1897

26:33

229

8 DELAWARE 1787* 1 1913 3:4≈

DISTRICT OF COLUMBIA

10:19 FLAG ADOPTED 1938

10 GEORGIA 1788* 4 1956

9 FLORIDA 1845 27 1900 2:3≈

2:3

12 IDAHO 1890 43 1927

11 HAWAII 1959 50 1845 1:2

26:33

13 ILLINOIS 1818 21 1970 3:5≈ ⌷

230

14 INDIAN.
1816
19
1917

26:33 ⌷

15 IOWA 1846 29 1921 3:4 ≈

16 KANSAS 1861 34 1963

3:5 ▭

18 LOUISIANA 1812 18 1912

17 KENTUCKY, COMMON-   10:19
WEALTH OF
1792 15 1963

2:3 ≈

20 MARYLAND 1788* 7 1904

26:33 ▭
19 MAINE 1820 23 1909

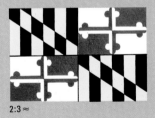

2:3 ≈

◄ 21 MASSACHUSETTS,
COMMONWEALTH OF 1788* 6 1971

3:5 ▭

22 MICHIGAN   1837   26   1911 ▶

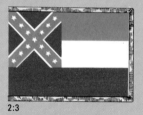

2:3 ≈

23 MINNESOTA   1858   32   1957

3:5

24 MISSISSIPPI   1817   20   1894

2:3

25 MISSOURI   1821   24   1913

7:12

26 MONTANA   1889   41   1905

5:6 ≈

27 NEBRASKA   1867   37   1925

3:5 ≈

28 NEVADA   1864   36   1929

2:3 ≈

232

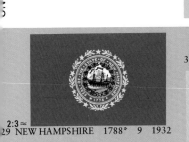

2:3 ≈
29 NEW HAMPSHIRE 1788* 9 1932

30 NEW JERSEY 1787* 3 1896

2:3 ≈

2:3 ≈
31 NEW MEXICO 1912 47 1925

32 NEW YORK 1788* 11 1901

10:19

3:4
33 NORTH CAROLINA 1789*
12 1885

34 NORTH
DAKOTA
1889 39 1911

26:33

36 OKLAHOMA 1907 46 1941

8:13
35 OHIO 1803 17 1902

2:3 ≈

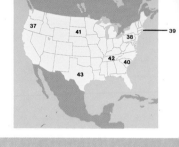

37 OREGON 1859 33 1925 **500:833** ≢

37 OREGON (REVERSE) **500:833**

27:37

38 PENNSYLVANIA, COMMON-
WEALTH OF 1787* 2 1907

39 RHODE ISL
AND PROVIDE
PLANTATIONS
STATE OF
1790*
13
1897

29:33

2:3 ≈

40 SOUTH CAROLINA 1788*
8 1861

41 SOUTH DAKOTA 1889 40 196

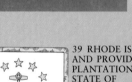

3:5

3:5

42 TENNESSEE 1796 16 1905

43 TEXAS 1845 28 1839

2:3

2:3 ≈

44 UTAH 1896 45 1913

45 VERMONT 1791 14 1923

2:3 ≈

2:3 ≈

46 VIRGINIA, COMMON-
WEALTH OF 1788* 10 1861

47 WASHINGTON 1889 42 1923

2:3

48 WEST VIRGINIA 1863 35
1929

10:19

49 WISCONSIN 1848 30 1913

26:33

7:10

50 WYOMING 1890 44 1917

235

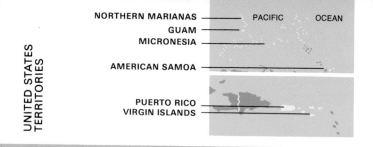

UNITED STATES TERRITORIES

NORTHERN MARIANAS —————
GUAM —————
MICRONESIA —————
AMERICAN SAMOA —————
PUERTO RICO —————
VIRGIN ISLANDS —————
PACIFIC   OCEAN

1:2 ≈

AMERICAN SAMOA
Officially hoisted 27 April 1960.

GUAM
Officially adopted 9 February 1948.

21:40

10:19

FEDERATED STATES OF MICRONESIA
Officially adopted 30 November 1978.

COMMONWEALTH OF NORTHERN MARIANAS ISLANDS
Officially adopted 31 March 1972.

20:39

2:3 ≈ COMMONWEALTH OF PUERTO RICO
In use since 22 December 1895;
officially adopted 24 July 1952.

VIRGIN ISLANDS OF THE UNITED STATES
Officially adopted 17 May 1921.

2:3 ≈

236

ROYAL ARMS

The Jordan state arms are similar to those formerly used by King Husayn of the Hijaz. The shield, helmet, and eagle of Saladin figure prominently. The inscription reads, ''The King of the Hashemite Kingdom of Jordan, al-Husayn-bin-Talal bin-Abdulla, Beseeches the Almighty for Aid and Success.''

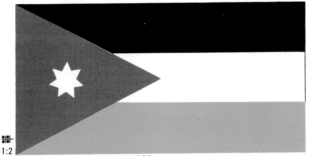

1:2

Officially adopted 16 April 1928.

The flag raised by Husayn in the Arab Revolt (see United Arab Emirates) has continued to the present day in slightly modified form as the flag of Jordan. The seven points of the star refer to the seven verses basic to Islamic belief which open the Quran.

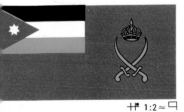

1:2 ≈ ⊏

1:2 ≈ ⊏

ROYAL FLAG   1:2

237

STATE ARMS

As part of the United Provinces of the River Plata—which became Argentina—the Eastern Strip (which became Uruguay) used the blue and white flag and gold sun which are still Argentine national symbols. In seeking independence from the United Provinces, General José Artigas and the Thirty and Three hoisted flags of

Officially
adopted
11 July 1830.

2:3

PRESIDENTIAL FLAG

3:5 ≈

The arms feature a balance for equality and justice, a horse and ox for liberty and plenty, and the hill of Montevideo as a symbol of strength. The arms evolved from those of the city of Montevideo in use in the 18th century.

horizontal stripes (blue-white-blue with a red diagonal and blue-white-red with a motto, respectively) which are still officially recognized by Uruguay as national symbols.

In 1828 when Uruguay finally achieved its independence, a new banner combining elements from the flags of Argentina and the United States was chosen. The nine blue stripes in that flag—and the nine blue and white stripes in the present flag—recall the nine departments into which Artigas had divided Uruguay.

238

CARIBBEAN SEA
★ Caracas
GUYANA
COLOMBIA
BRAZIL

STATE ARMS

The flag of Venezuela was first hoisted on the soil of America on 12 March 1806 by the leader in the independence movement, Francisco de Miranda. There is a tradition that the blue and red horizontal stripes were borrowed from the flag of Haiti, the place from which Miranda's invasion of Venezuela was launched. Never-

Officially adopted 19 February 1954.

2:3

2:3

SUCRE   3:4 ≈

theless, a more likely source of the colors is the flag proposed by the leaders of the abortive Venezuelan revolution of 1797, Manuel Gual and José María España. Its stripes of white, blue, red, and yellow stood respectively for the whites, blacks, mulattoes, and Indians. The first use of the stars—one for each of the original provinces—dates from 1817; they became a permanent part of the flag in 1859. Since independence in 1830, Venezuela's flag has undergone only minor modifications—in its coat of arms and the arrangement of its stars.

STATE ARMS

On 29 September 1945 a design dating from at least 1940 became the official flag of the Democratic Republic of Viet-Nam. That flag differed only slightly from the one that replaced it in 1955 after ten years of struggle to preserve national independence and unity. Instead of the regular five-pointed star which is now

Officially hoisted 2 July 1976.

2:3

In the state arms of the Democratic Republic of Viet-Nam decreed in 1956, the central portion recalls the design of the state flag. Surrounding it is a wreath of rice, the chief crop of this largely agricultural land. The will to industrialize is reflected in the cogwheel at the bottom. Instead of a motto, the name of the state is written on the ribbon that binds the sheaves of rice. The only change instituted in the arms with the organization of the Socialist Republic of Viet-Nam was introduction of the new name on the ribbon.

official, the original flag had a wide-angle star—that is, one in which the inner diameter equaled one-half the outer diameter.

In 1960 the South Viet-Nam National Liberation Front was organized. On 8 June 1969 its flag became official for the Republicof South Viet-Nam, which six years later overthrew the Republic of Viet-Nam—a government supported by the United States. A year later north and south Viet-Nam were unified under the flag of the Democratic Republic. The flag of the Republic of South Viet-Nam, which had been of the same design except that its background consisted of two (red over light-blue) stripes, disappeared.

STATE ARMS

Yemen experienced a revolution in 1962 which completely altered its national symbols. The red stripe in the new flag is the revolutionary spirit which motivated the Yemeni people in almost a decade of civil war that secured the establishment of the republic. Black is for the dark days of the past, and white expresses hope in

Officially
hoisted ca.
1 November
1962.

2:3

In 1958 Egypt and Syria created a unitary state, the United Arab Republic, and Iraq and Jordan formed a federation, the Arab Union. Both had distinctive flags. The same year Yemen and the United Arab Republic confederated under the name United Arab States. Because of the loose ties between the two member states, the United Arab States did not have a distinctive flag of its own. However, the United Arab Republic flag (with one star omitted) was adopted as the flag of Yemen after its monarchy was overthrown.

a better future. The single star symbolizes unity and independence.
An eagle representing the strength of the Yemeni people overshadows a ribbon with the name of the state inscribed on it. The coffee plant on the shield is appropriate, mocha coffee being named for the Yemeni city of Al-Mukha. Below the coffee is a representation of the Marib Dam, an important structure in the national irrigation system from the time of its building in the seventh century B.C. to the time of its collapse in the sixth century A.D.

171 AL YAMAN YEMEN

STATE ARMS

The oppressive colonial and feudal regimes in Yemen's past are reflected in the flag's black stripe. White is for peace and red for revolution; the light blue triangle represents the people of the nation under the leadership of the National Liberation Front—symbolized by the red star. The flag is based on the red-white-black banner of

Usage initiated ca. 30 November 1967.

2:3

In the early 19th century Yemen covered much of the territory now divided between the Yemen Arab Republic and the People's Democratic Republic of Yemen. In 1972 and again in 1979 the countries announced their intention to reunite under a single government and flag.
The People's Democratic Republic of Yemen is sometimes called Yemen (Aden) or Democratic Yemen or South Yemen to differentiate it from its western neighbor, commonly referred to as Yemen or Yemen (San'a).

the National Liberation Front, the organization which overthrew local rulers and eventually forced the British to recognize the independence of the country. The flag of the Front had been based on the Arab Revolt Flag (see Egypt). The party flag was modified by the addition to it of a triangle and star to become the national flag.
The Yemeni coat of arms follows the pattern in use by the United Arab Republic at the time Yemen received independence (see Iraq). The golden eagle of Saladin grasps a plaque with the name of the state.

STATE ARMS

After years of civil war and psychological dependence on its colonial heritage, the Congo was Africanized by President Joseph Mobutu—in part by changing names and national symbols.

The background color of the new national flag—a symbol of hope and faith in the future—was originally

Officially
hoisted ca.
20 November
1971.

2:3 ≈

PRESIDENTIAL FLAG

3:4 ≈ 🏳

The arms and presidential flag show traditional weapons, the lance and arrow, framed by a palm branch and elephant tusk. The national motto ("Justice, Peace, Work") appears below the representation of a stone.

used in the emblem of Mobutu's Popular Movement of the Revolution, as was the central emblem. The arm and flaming torch graphically express the revolutionary spirit the nation aspires to and the red flames honor the nation's martyrs. The original flag proposal included a narrow red horizontal stripe recalling the blood of martyrs and a blue one to symbolize the rivers and lakes of the country. The presidential flag is displayed by the chief executive in his capacity as captain general of the Zaire Armed Forces. He also flies the national flag on his automobile.

243

STATE ARMS

The eagle of liberty in the arms and flag reflects the aspiration to rise to greater things and the ability of the nation to overcome problems. In the arms the eagle hovers over a heraldic representation of Victoria Falls, its white waters streaming over black rock. The black shield, suggesting the African population of the country, is a

Officially hoisted 24 October 1964.

2:3

PRESIDENTIAL FLAG

2:3

The national flag is based on the colors found in the flag of the United National Independence Party which spearheaded the struggle for freedom from Britain.

link to the Zambezi River from which the name Zambia is derived. The shield and eagle are adaptations from the arms of the Colony of Northern Rhodesia dating to 1927.

Emblems of mineral riches, wildlife, and agricultural produce frame the shield. Rather than heraldic beasts or legendary figures from the past, Zambia chose as supporters the common man and woman of the nation.

The green field of the flag and its orange stripe are intended to stand for natural resources and mineral wealth. Black is for the Zambian people and red is a token of their struggle to achieve freedom.

STATE ARMS

ZAMBIA

BOTSWANA

Salisbury ✶

INDIAN OCEAN

Until 1979 the country was known as Rhodesia (prior to 1965, Southern Rhodesia). The Latin motto in the arms refers to the original namesake of the country, 19th century British imperialist Cecil Rhodes: it translates as ''May [Rhodesia] Be Worthy of the Name.'' The crest of the arms is a representation of the carved soap-

⣿
1:2

Officially hoisted 11 November 1968.

PRESIDENTIAL FLAG   7:10

The election of April 1979 for a black government—or the civil war currently being waged—may lead to changes in the national flag.

stone bird found in the ruins of the ancient city of Zimbabwe.

Prior to its choice for the flag, green had been considered the national color because of its use by various sports teams. It alludes to the agricultural basis of the Rhodesian economy. The arms, granted by royal warrant on 11 August 1924, have a gold pickaxe symbolic of mining and sable antelopes to recall the wildlife of Rhodesia. The shield has the lion and thistles originally found in the family arms of Cecil Rhodes, who helped to bring the territory under the sway of the Union Jack in 1890.

INTERNATIONAL FLAGS, SIGNALS AND PENNANTS

Since World War II there has been an enormous growth in the number of flags with international significance. Partly this is a reflection of the growth of international and regional organizations, such as the United Nations and the South Pacific Commission and military alliances such as the North Atlantic Treaty Organization.

Three of the best known and most widely used international flags are represented here. The Geneva Convention of 1863 provided for the distinctive Red Cross flag as a symbol of its humanitarian efforts. There also exist flags bearing the other recognized Geneva Convention symbols—the Red Crescent (for Muslim countries) and Red Lion and Sun (Iran).

The flag of the Olympic Games emphasizes the five continents linked in the peaceful competition for athletic achievement. The flag of the United Nations, adopted on 20 October 1947, speaks of the main goal of that organization—peace throughout the world. The International Code of Signals, most recently refined in 1969, finds its usage decreasing in an era of sophisticated electronic communications.

UNITED NATIONS   2:3

OLYMPIC GAMES   2:3

RED CROSS   1:1

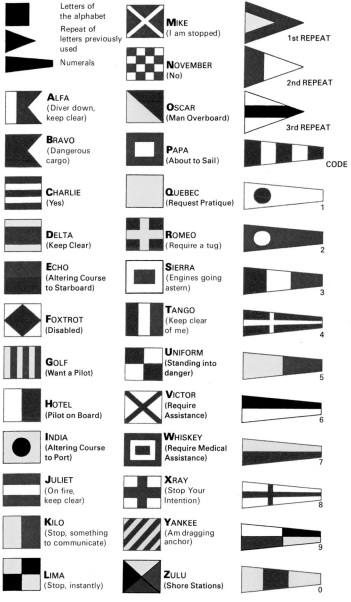

Letters of the alphabet

Repeat of letters previously used

Numerals

ALFA (Diver down, keep clear)

BRAVO (Dangerous cargo)

CHARLIE (Yes)

DELTA (Keep Clear)

ECHO (Altering Course to Starboard)

FOXTROT (Disabled)

GOLF (Want a Pilot)

HOTEL (Pilot on Board)

INDIA (Altering Course to Port)

JULIET (On fire, keep clear)

KILO (Stop, something to communicate)

LIMA (Stop, instantly)

MIKE (I am stopped)

NOVEMBER (No)

OSCAR (Man Overboard)

PAPA (About to Sail)

QUEBEC (Request Pratique)

ROMEO (Require a tug)

SIERRA (Engines going astern)

TANGO (Keep clear of me)

UNIFORM (Standing into danger)

VICTOR (Require Assistance)

WHISKEY (Require Medical Assistance)

XRAY (Stop Your Intention)

YANKEE (Am dragging anchor)

ZULU (Shore Stations)

1st REPEAT

2nd REPEAT

3rd REPEAT

CODE

1

2

3

4

5

6

7

8

9

0

ADDITIONAL TEXTS

both land and sea.

Other Bahamian flags follow a general British pattern, recalling two-and-one-half centuries under British rule. The mace in the flag of the prime minister, a symbol of parliamentary authority, indicates the peaceful evolution of the country to independence. The coat of arms has native fauna—the marlin, flamingo, and conch shell—as well as symbols of its pleasant climate (the sun), beautiful water (the waves), and vegetation (palm fronds). The landing of Columbus on San Salvador (now Watlings Island) in the Bahamas on 12 October 1492 is reflected in the principal emblem on the shield, Columbus's flagship.

13 BELGIUM

colors were used in various military colors of complicated design. The simple Belgian Tricolor was first hoisted on 26 August 1830 by Edouard Ducpétiaux and Lucien Jottrand on the city hall in Brussels. The three equal stripes were undoubtedly inspired by the French Tricolor.

The provisional government issued its recognition of a national flag the following January, indicating that the colors red, yellow, and black were to be placed vertically.

The same colors were introduced into a war ensign in 1950. Its saltire derives from the cross of Burgundy which characterized flags of Belgium when it was the Spanish (later Austrian) Netherlands, prior to the 19th century.

14 BELIZE

number of years.

That flag contains an adaptation of the coat of arms granted to the country on 28 January 1907 when it was known as British Honduras. The blacks who served as supporters in the original arms have been replaced by men of different races to reflect the ethnic diversity of Belize, and the Union Jack has been omitted from the shield. Although referring to British protection, the Latin motto which translates as "I Flourish in the Shade" has been retained.

The flag flown by the common people omits the arms: it is simply a white disk on blue. The flag badge defacing the British Blue Ensign as used on state ships is an adaptation of the official arms.

The flag badge and both versions of the arms bear tools—a squaring axe, paddle, beating axe, and a two-man crosscut saw—employed in the logging industry which originally attracted the British to the area.

21 BRUNEI

symbolizing justice, tranquillity, prosperity, and peace. The central mast is an emblem of stable and just government, while the hands on either side are pledges of the people's dedication to the government and of the state's promise to provide well-being, peace, and prosperity.

The Islamic faith of the people is indicated by the crescent. It is inscribed in Arabic "Always Render Service by the Guidance of God," while the ribbon at the bottom bears the phrase "Brunei, Gate of Peace."

22 BULGARIA

flags including those of Yugoslavia and Czechoslovakia. The Bulgarians see the colors of their flag respectively as symbols of peace, love, and freedom; wealth from the soil; and the courage of the Bulgarian people. Agriculture and industry are reflected in the wheat and cogwheel of the arms. Communism is symbolized by the red star, while the date 1944 marks the liberation of Bulgaria from fascism.

While the lion has officially served as an emblem of Bulgaria since 1879, it also was known as early as the late 14th century when it appeared on coins issued by a Bulgarian czar, Ivan Shishman.

26 CANADA

buildings flew this flag, although a large number of citizens considered the British Union Jack as the proper Canadian national flag.

Following World War I, in which many Canadians participated, government authorities sought a complete and appropriate new coat of arms. The arms, granted by royal warrant on 21 November 1921, provided a new shield for the Canadian Red Ensign. When the new design was actually introduced, the Order in Council (dated 26 January 1924) provided for use of the flag on Canadian government buildings. This was reaffirmed in 1945, but by then growing segments of the population had expressed their discontent with the basic design.

Whether or not Canada should formally adopt a national flag of its own and, if so, what its design should be were questions touching on the deepest sentiments of the people.

Led by Prime Minister Lester Pearson, the forces favoring a new flag eventually won the day in 1964 after a bitter parliamentary struggle. The flag chosen displays the maple leaf, a symbol of Canada in use for at least a century. Red and white, the national colors, had been incorporated in the 1921 coat of arms, red symbolizing the sacrifice Canadians had made in World War I and white suggesting the snowy north.

The arms include quarterings for England, Scotland, Ireland, and France—the original homelands of much of the Canadian population. The

motto, a biblical adaptation, means "From Sea to Sea." British influence in Canadian symbolism remains strong and the Union Jack has been officially recognized as a symbol of Canada's links to the Commonwealth.

30 CHINA

canton became the Chinese war ensign. This "White Sun in Blue Sky over Red Land" became the civil and state flag on 8 October 1928 and in 1940 was also adopted by the Japanese-sponsored KMT Republic of China regime.

Red has long been regarded as the national color of the Han, the ethnic group constituting the overwhelming majority of the Chinese population. The blue of the flag stands for equality and justice; the white is a symbol of fraternity and frankness. White, blue, and red also correspond to the Three Principles of the People enunciated by the father of the Republic of China, Dr. Sun Yat-sen— popular well-being, popular government, and popular sovereignty (or welfare, democracy, and nationalism).

38 DENMARK

design may be linked with the war flag of the Holy Roman Emperors, who considered Denmark a vassal state. Their red war flag charged with the white cross of Christianity can be documented not only in the "Danish Marches" (i.e., Denmark) but in other parts of the Empire.

National flags in the modern sense did not come into existence until the American and French Revolutions of the late 18th century, and the Dannebrog did not have official status as a national flag on land until 1854. Moreover, there have been variations over the centuries in the exact form of the flag used for different purposes. Nevertheless, it must be recognized that the white cross on red flag has been the chief Danish symbol for at least 600 years. A coin suggests that it may even date from the second half of the 12th century, while plain red flags are known to have been used in the Baltic Sea as early as the ninth century.

The Dannebrog exists in two forms—the *splitflag*, since 1625 officially reserved for the navy and royal institutions, and the rectangular version, for private display on land and at sea. Since 1690 special badges have been added to indicate a particular government or private institution.

The island of Greenland is part of the Danish kingdom, with internal self-government dating from 1 May 1979. A flag for Greenland was in the process of being designed at the time of writing (April 1979).

39 GERMANY

had become popular following their use in the uniform worn in 1813 by the Lützow Free Corps, during the Wars of Liberation which marked a decisive turn in German history toward nationalism and unification. At that time people believed that these were the traditional colors of Germany. Their tricolor arrangement (whether in horizontal or vertical stripes) was undoubtedly inspired by the French Tricolor. The National Assembly which gathered in St.Paul's Church in Frankfurt in 1848 attempted to create a German Confederation. The flag of its ships—in actual use from 1848 to 1852—was the black-red-gold flag with a black double-headed eagle on a gold canton.

The colors have had a long historical tradition in Germany. For example, since the 13th century the heraldic arms and banner of the Holy Roman Empire, which was essentially a German state through most of its existence, displayed a gold field with a black eagle. Its tongue, beak, and feet were usually red—as in the current official arms of the Federal Republic. The eagle had been adopted because the legions of the original Roman Empire displayed vexilloids (flag-like standards) consisting of a gold eagle at the top of a pole.

50 SPAIN

Concerning the gold shield of Aragon with its four red stripes—an emblem used today by several Spanish regions for their local flags—there is a charming legend. In the ninth century Charles the Bald, grandson of Charlemagne, supposedly visited his wounded ally, Count Wilfred I of Aragon. The story has Charles dip four fingers in Wilfred's blood, then draw them down his plain gold shield. In fact, there is no proven use of the arms prior to King Ramon Berenguer IV in the early 12th century.

The golden chains on the red shield of Navarre refer to the Battle of Navas Tolosa on 16 July 1212. The arms of Granada—a pomegranate (*granada* in Spanish) on silver—is based on the personal emblem of King Henry IV (1454–1474).

The overseas expansion of Spain and the influence of its civilization on a large part of the world are manifested in the pillars of Hercules which flank the shield. The Latin motto reads ''[There Is] More Beyond.'' Behind the head of the eagle of St.John which supports the shield is the motto ''One, Great, Free.'' Below the eagle are a yoke and a bundle of arrows, symbols of the Catholic monarchs Isabella and Ferdinand.

52 FIJI

Ensign with the full coat of arms in the fly, usually on a white disk. The shield of the arms alone, rather than the full achievement, was preferred for the new flag as being more readily distinguishable at a distance. The dove with a branch of olive and the national motto (''Fear God and Honor the King'') are symbols used by the Kingdom of Fiji (1871–1874) before it became a British colony.

The coat of arms of modern Fiji was granted by royal warrant on 4 July 1908 and confirmed on 30 September

1970. The cross of St.George, patron saint of England, separates local agricultural produce—sugar cane, a coconut palm, and bananas. Another symbol of England, the rampant gold lion on red, appears in the chief of the shield, holding between its paws a cocoa pod. Fiji warriors in the traditional mulberry tree bark kilt hold a spear and pineapple club respectively. The crest is a Fijian canoe with an outrigger, somewhat similar to the one that appears in the flag of Guam. In the standard of the Governor-General the name Fiji appears on a *tabua* or whale's tooth. This is a traditional gift of welcome in the islands.

54 FRANCE

a French national color during the 15th century, chiefly under the influence of Joan of Arc and the House of Orleans.

A new flag was realized in the law adopted on 24 October 1790: it was white throughout three-quarters of its field, but the canton bore vertical stripes of red-white-blue with borders of the same colors. In 1794 a committee recommended the flag in its present form, in calling for "an ensign formed completely of the three national colors, [a] simple [design] as is appropriate for republican morals, ideas, and principles."

The Napoleonic Wars firmly established the Tricolor as the flag of France, although the white flag was brought back briefly under the Restoration (1814–1815 and 1815–1830). The July Revolution of 1830 saw the publication on 2 August of a decree signed by King Louis Philippe: "The French nation takes up again its colors. There shall not be worn any cockade other than the tricolored cockade." When revolutionaries demanded in 1848 the replacement of the Tricolor by a flag of plain red, the poet Alphonse de Lamartine exclaimed, "The Tricolor has made a tour of the world with the name, the

glory, and the liberty of the Fatherland!" That year a red rosette was ordered to be added to the top of the pole bearing the national flag and for two weeks the order of the stripes was blue-red-white, but the original Tricolor was soon restored. The plain red flag again failed to challenge the Tricolor successfully in 1871, although it was the chief symbol of the Commune in Paris.

A special version of the Tricolor was established on 17 May 1853 for use at sea. It has stripes in relative proportions of 30:33:37, which supposedly produces the visual impression of equality between the different colors when seen from a distance.

73 ISRAEL

In 1897 this flag was submitted at the World Zionist Organization conference in Basel by the Boston delegate, Isaac Harris. Other Jews had conceived of similar designs. The flag quickly became accepted as the Zionist emblem, and in 1948 it was adopted by the State of Israel.

The state arms reflect other ancient Jewish symbols. The name of the state and the olive branches of prosperity frame a candelabra such as the Romans carried off in triumph after the destruction of Jerusalem in 70 A.D. The combination of the candelabra and branches is mentioned in Zechariah 4:2–3 in the Bible.

74 ITALY

The same colors were introduced into a civil flag by the neighboring Cispadane Federation. On 7 January 1797 it adopted a horizontal tricolor—the first authentic Italian national flag. That flag had a coat of arms, but a plain green-white-red vertical tricolor was made official on 11 May 1798 for the Cisalpine Republic, which amalgamated the Transpadane and Cispadane states. Italy's Tricolor went through further political and military struggles before it achieved universal recognition by all Italians as their national flag. A landmark was reached on 23 March 1848 when King Charles Albert of Sardinia ordered his troops to carry the Italian Tricolor into battle. With the arms of the House of Savoy in the center, this flag flew on the proclamation of Italy as an independent kingdom on 18 March 1861. The most recent form of the flag was established in 1946, when the monarchy was abolished and its coat of arms removed from the flag.

90 LUXEMBOURG

and civil aviation and dates from 1972. In the form of a military color, it has since 1853 been the army flag of Luxembourg.

The national flag was first established (in the form now used) on 12 June 1845. The source of the colors is the shield; previously they had been arranged in various ways as unofficial Luxembourg tricolors. The flag is only coincidentally similar to the flag of the Netherlands, whose shade of blue is somewhat darker.

115 JAPAN

sun and the moon. The intended symbolism of these two celestial objects is clear: just as they shed their light both day and night over all parts of the world, so the emperor illuminates his nation at all times.

The tradition of a banner with a sun and/or moon is strong in Japan because of the legend that the imperial line was established by the progeny of goddess Amaterasu-Omikami, "Heaven-Shining Great Deity." Examples of the use of these flags can be traced through the centuries, until eventually the emperor adopted a flag bearing a chrysanthemum and the sun flag became representative of the nation as a whole.

The adoption of a national flag, corresponding to those of other countries both in form and function, was precipitated by the arrival of American Commodore Matthew C. Perry in

1853. Led by Nariakira, Lord of Satsuma, those favoring the Sun Disk flag over other designs were successful in having it recognized as the Japanese ensign on 5 August 1854. Following the Restoration of 3 January 1868, whereby the emperor regained powers that had long been controlled by the Shogunate, the sun flag was extended to further uses by the law of 27 February 1870.

The white of the flag is seen as an expression of purity and integrity, while red suggests fervor, sincerity, and enthusiasm. Japan's very name means "Source of the Sun" and thus the flag manifests the country directly in graphic terms. The war flag and ensign, adopted on 3 November 1889, is a further expression of this basic symbolism.

116 NORWAY

blue were seen as symbols of liberty, based on their use in the French, British, and American flags.

Norway had been under Danish rule from 1380 to 1814, but in the latter year the victorious powers in the Napoleonic Wars decreed that it should be united with Sweden. Norwegian resistance to this union resulted in its obtaining the right to a distinctive flag of its own, but for the next eight decades a struggle was carried on to make this a "clean" or purely Norwegian flag.

The basic Norwegian flag was suggested by Frederik Meltzer, a member of parliament, and was adopted in 1821. At first its usage was restricted to waters near Norway; later a union badge formed by the combination of the Swedish and Norwegian crosses was added in the canton. When the struggle to achieve unrestricted use of the clean flag was crowned with success in 1898, it presaged the separation of the two kingdoms and the complete independence of Norway on 7 June 1905.

dence of Pakistan in 1947.

The flag of the Muslim League was green, long considered the chief religious color of Islam. The Muslim star and crescent were featured in the center of that flag. But the party flag was not adopted directly by the nation; a white stripe was added at the hoist to represent minorities living in the state.

Following British tradition, the presidential standard is dark blue: the name of the country is inscribed on it below the crescent. Above the motto "Faith, Unity, Discipline" in the national arms appear the products on which the national economy relies— cotton, tea, wheat, and jute. The flowers in the wreath are narcissi.

The Pakistani national colors are prominent in the flag of Azad Jammu and Kashmir; the orange stands for its Hindu minority. The stripes suggest the valleys and rivers of this territory which, although under Pakistani administration since the war with India in 1947–1948, has not been annexed to Pakistan.

121 PARAGUAY

the King of Spain. The Star of May in the national arms recalls the date of independence, 14 May 1811. Defense of national liberty is symbolized by the lion guarding the liberty cap on the Treasury seal whose motto proclaims "Peace and Justice." Use of the seal makes the Paraguayan flag unique—the only national flag in the world with a different design on either side.

141 SINGAPORE

ted on 25 March 1911. The original arms of Singapore (dating from 1948) contained lions on both the shield and crest.

The present arms and flag both date from 1959 when self-government was introduced. The official interpretation is that the "crescent represents a young country on the ascent in its ideals of establishing democracy, peace, progress, justice, and equality as indicated by the five stars."

There are also official explanations for the symbolism of the red and white colors. The former stands for universal brotherhood and the latter for purity and virtue.

Singapore was to have become part of the new Federation of Malaysia on 31 August 1963, but the delay in the creation of that state led to Singapore's unilateral declaration of independence on that date. It was subsequently part of Malaysia—from 16 September 1963 until again becoming independent on 9 August 1965—without any change in the 1959 flag.

142 SOLOMON ISLANDS

Eastern, Western, Malaita, Central, and Eastern Outer Islands District. They are surrounded by blue for the waters of the sea. The yellow and green stand for the sun and the land. Several of the same elements appear in the coat of arms granted when the Solomon Islands became independent on 7 July 1978. (Earlier, similar arms had been granted on 24 September 1956 by Queen Elizabeth II.) The turtles are for the Western District and the frigate bird for the Eastern District. The sandfordi eagle stands for the Malaita District, while the crossed spears, dancing shield, bow, and arrow represent the Central District. A two-headed frigate bird, the saltwater crocodile, a shark, a native boat, and the national motto complete the design.

148 FINLAND

unofficial flags and flag proposals. Others chose the colors white and blue, which the poet Zachris Topelius suggested would symbolize the snows and the lakes of Finland.

The first use of a blue cross on a white field dates from 4 March 1861 when the Nyland Yacht Club received approval from the czar to use such a flag with the arms of Nyland County in the upper hoist corner. This flag, similar to one created in 1846 by the Imperial Russian Yacht Society, was so popular in the Gulf of Finland that it came to be unofficially recognized as the flag of Finland.

During the struggle for Finland's independence and the civil war which followed it (1917–1918), the first national flag was an interpretation in flag form of the arms, while the second one had the Scandinavian cross, rendered in the four popular Finnish colors. The basic pattern of the current civil flag and ensign and of the state flag and ensign was established on 29 May 1918, although there have been variations in the color shades and artistic renditions over the years.

151 SWEDEN

Sweden from 1250 to 1363, a combination dating back at least to 1448. In the center are the arms of the families of the current king, the Vasas and the Bernadottes.

References dating back at least to 1449 mention Swedish use of a shied with gold cross on a blue field. In 1569 King Johan III indicated his desire that the yellow cross found in the Swedish arms should also be incorporated in banners and flags of all kinds in his realm. The inspiration for the national flag may have been the result of combining the Swedish national armorial colors with the cross flag already long in use in Denmark, with which Sweden was united from 1397 to 1523.

In the Flag Act of 1663 provision was made for the two basic flags still in use today—the rectangular and the swallowtailed versions. During much of the 19th century Swedish flags had a union emblem in the canton to indicate that the king of Sweden was also the sovereign of Norway.

165 UNITED STATES

country. In 1795 Congress decided to add a new star and stripe for the two states that had joined the Union since its formation. That 15-star, 15-stripe flag was the first to be called the Star-Spangled Banner—a name popularized in the poem by Francis Scott Key which, in 1931, was recognized as the words to the national anthem.

The further addition of states made that flag obsolete. Peter Wendover, the representative of New York in Congress, deserves credit as the man whose foresight preserved both the original harmony of the flag and the concept of honoring new states. Rather than reverting to 13 stars and 13 stripes or, at the other extreme, continuing to add one star and one stripe for each new state, he recommended—and the Congress accepted—the concept which is still part of American law. The basic design of the flag would henceforth be 13 equal horizontal stripes honoring the original states; the canton would be blue containing one white star for each state. Over the years this has produced a total of 27 different American flags—if one disregards the endless variety of unofficial (and sometimes quite incorrect) designs. The popularity of the basic design is seen in the fact that many flags have been based on it, including those of several states and of the rebellious Confederate States of America (1860–1865).

The federal system of government is also reflected in the motto of the national arms, "One Out of Many." The blue in the shield stands for Congress, the supreme governmental authority under the Articles of Confederation which was replaced by the present constitution in 1787. The olive branch and arrows declare the power of Congress to decide matters of peace and war.